THE BASICS OF
PERFORMANCE
MEASUREMENT

2nd Edition

THE BASICS OF
PERFORMANCE
MEASUREMENT

2nd Edition

Jerry L. Harbour

CRC Press
Taylor & Francis Group
Boca Raton   London   New York

CRC Press is an imprint of the
Taylor & Francis Group, an **informa** business

A PRODUCTIVITY PRESS BOOK

Productivity Press
Taylor & Francis Group
270 Madison Avenue
New York, NY 10016

© 2009 by Jerry L. Harbour
Productivity Press is an imprint of Taylor & Francis Group, an Informa business

No claim to original U.S. Government works

Printed in the United States of America on acid-free paper
10 9 8 7 6 5 4 3 2 1

International Standard Book Number: 978-1-4398-0249-6 (Paperback)

Library of Congress Cataloging-in-Publication Data

Harbour, Jerry L.
    The basics of performance measurement / Jerry L. Harbour. -- 2nd ed.
        p. cm.
    Includes bibliographical references and index.
    ISBN 978-1-4398-0249-6
    1. Performance standards. 2. Performance--Evaluation. I. Title.

HF5549.5.P35H37 2009
658.3'125--dc22   2009008454

Visit the Taylor & Francis Web site at
http://www.taylorandfrancis.com

and the Productivity Press Web site at
http://www.productivitypress.com

Contents

Preface

Following the publication of my fourth book, *The Performance Paradox—Understanding the Real Drivers that Critically Affect Outcomes*, the good folks at Productivity Press suggested that I update and revise *The Basics of Performance Measurement*. I wholeheartedly agreed with their recommendation.

The "little yellow book," as I fondly call the first edition, was originally published in 1997. Despite a plethora of books related to performance measurement that have come to market since, the little book has held its own for over a decade now, chugging out respectable sales month after month and year after year. Yet despite the book's current relevancy—some things just do not change—and continued sales, I freely admit that it is time for a bit of an update and facelift.

Accordingly, I have refreshed and expanded some of the existing chapters in the original publication and considerably rewritten a few others. I have also added two new chapters, one on units of measurement and another on how to better "interpret" what has been measured and translate those measurement-related interpretations into actionable knowledge. In turn, the publisher has added more "size" to the little book's format and given it a whole new look and cover.

Although I have certainly aged since the original publication of *The Basics of Performance Measurement*, I have also become a bit wiser and perhaps even a shade smarter about the whole subject of performance in general and the tenets of performance measurement in particular. It is this added "wisdom" that I have attempted to embed in this second edition of *The Basics of Performance Measurement*, a book that is hopefully even more relevant, usable, and wiser today than it was when it was originally published over a decade ago. So as always, please enjoy!

1

Performance Measurement

> You can't understand, manage, or improve what you don't measure.

Whether you use Six Sigma, Lean Six Sigma, business process reengineering, total quality management, continuous improvement, or cycle time reduction, the basic goal is essentially the same: to do more better and faster with less. A critical enabler and success factor in each of these common improvement endeavors is the ability to quantitatively measure performance. As the saying goes, "You can't understand, manage, or improve what you don't measure." High-performing organizations seem to understand this basic principle and have developed highly effective performance measurement systems within their respective organizations, irrespective of particular organizational affinity.

> A critical enabler in achieving desired performance goals is the ability to quantitatively measure performance.

How would you respond, for example, if the chief executive officer (CEO) of your company challenged you to cut the average cycle time of a particularly troublesome and costly process by 50% over the next 12 months? One possible avenue would be to brainstorm a few ideas and immediately implement one or two of those ideas. At the end of the 12-month period, you could go back to the CEO and assure him that the cycle time had indeed been cut in half. If the discerning CEO happened to ask you for some positive proof to back up your assertion, you might be surprised— was it not obvious? Often standards such as ISO 9001 require documentation of an improvement effort.

A different and more defensible approach to the CEO's challenge would be to:

- First establish the baseline cycle time of the current process; that is, you would measure the "as is"—in this case the current average cycle time is 8 days.
- Next calculate your goal: a 50% reduction in cycle time. This would determine your targeted goal for the coming year, which in this case is 4 days.
- Determine the gap or delta between the current cycle time and targeted cycle time. To reach your desired goal, you must somehow eliminate 4 days from the present process.
- Develop and implement a process improvement solution. This represents the "means" of how you will actually reach the "end" or your targeted goal of 4 days.
- Finally, throughout the year measure the current cycle time. Such measures, whether on a continuous or periodic basis, help you track the progress that you are making toward achieving and maintaining the desired 4-day goal.

At the end of the 1-year period, you can now graphically show the CEO your progress with a chart like the one illustrated in Figure 1.1. You could

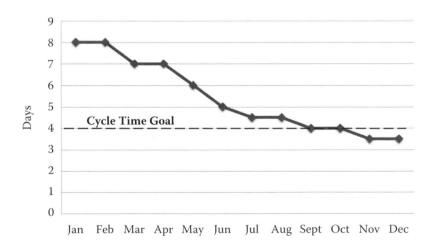

FIGURE 1.1
Performance measurement graph.

state that 12 months ago, the average cycle time was 8 days. You would then show the CEO the monthly progress chart and proudly announce that the current cycle time is 3.5 days. This measured and documented performance improvement effort actually represents a 56% reduction in cycle time, rather than the targeted 50%!

The first approach, which is still unfortunately fairly common, is based on opinion and speculation. The second is based on fact and actual measurement. Increasingly, companies are opting for the latter approach. They are managing their improvement efforts and the performance of their organizations on the basis of fact and concrete evidence, not subjective opinion. And those evidence-based facts are being driven by quantitatively measuring performance; that is, companies are using performance measures to drive and achieve desired performance levels. They are also using such measures as a means to delve deeper into a better understanding of their respective organizations.

One company, for example, that has several call centers has developed a fairly sophisticated performance measurement system for assessing customer service. Each month, a "cumulative average service score" is collected at each call center and sent to company headquarters, where it is tabulated and graphically plotted. A representative plot of the collected information from each call center is illustrated in Figure 1.2.

Seeing the plot for the first time, a newly hired senior manager wonders aloud what the variation within each call center is. For example, do individual customer service scores cluster closely around the calculated average, thus indicating that customer service is fairly consistent and reliable within a particular call center? Or do average customer service scores vary widely, suggesting an inconsistent, highly variable, and "hit and miss" customer service quality?

Because each call center already collects individual service scores and simply averages them together to calculate a cumulative average service score, it is a relatively easy task to determine variation about that average by calculating a standard deviation. A standard deviation is simply a measure of how "spread out" your data are from the average. Think of it as a measure of how much variability there is in a process or system. Low standard deviations mean little dispersion or variation, while high values indicate just the opposite.

Armed with such knowledge, the company plots average cumulative service scores on the y, or vertical axis of a graph, and associated standard deviations on the x, or horizontal axis, as illustrated in Figure 1.3. Viewing

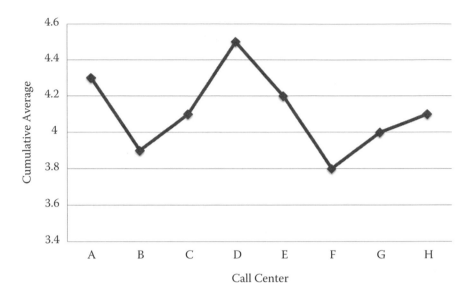

FIGURE 1.2
Average cumulative call center service scores.

the graphical plot, much can be learned about the variability of customer service within the various individual call centers. Note that some call centers have good overall service scores with low associated variability, as indicated by low standard deviations. This combination indicates that customer service is fairly consistent within these call centers.

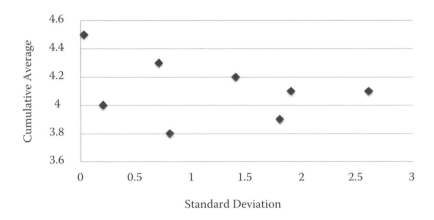

FIGURE 1.3
Average service scores versus standard deviations.

Conversely, other call centers (some with almost the same average overall service scores as other call centers) have much higher standard deviations. Such scores at these call centers mean that some customers are getting great customer service while others are getting very poor service. If the company's goal is to provide consistently high-quality service to all customers, then at certain call centers they have some definite work to do.

Often, and as just illustrated, a bit of additional processing of collected performance measures can tell us a great deal about the performance of our respective organizations. The good news is that such derived greater understanding is normally relatively easy and cheap to acquire and does not entail collecting ever larger amounts of data.

Collecting performance measures can also help us make better and more optimal economic decisions. For example, one company that assembles various components into a final "high-tech" product puts each new employee who will work on the assembly line through an extensive and costly 3-week training program. With a fairly high employee turnover rate, training costs within the company are quite high.

When a new director of training for the company asks why the new employee training program lasts 3 weeks, she is told that it has always been that long and, in addition, trainees come out of the 3-week training session well qualified and ready to go to work. Knowing, however, that skill acquisition and associated gains in performance often follow an S shaped curve form, such that a point is reached where additional training results in only marginal gains at best, she is interested when the flat top of the S-curve, called an asymptote, is actually reached within the 3-week training period.

As illustrated in Figure 1.4, testing student skill levels on a daily basis reveals that gains in performance actually top out at about the 11- to 12-day mark. Subsequent training and practice trials add little benefit in actually increasing trainee performance. Accordingly, the director of training decides to reduce the 15-day training program to 12 days. The 20% reduction in course length will translate into sizable cost savings given the high number of training courses that are delivered each year.

As illustrated in the previous three examples, companies are discovering that performance measures can help any organization to:

- Determine where they are, that is, establish an initial baseline "as is" performance level
- Establish goals on the basis of their current performance

- Determine the gap or delta between a set of desired goals and current performance levels
- Track progress in achieving desired performance goals and ensure that such goals are maintained
- Compare and benchmark their competitors' performance levels with their own
- Assess variation within a system or process and help control such variation within predetermined boundaries
- Identify problem areas and possible problem causes
- Make more informed performance-, cost-, and fact-based decisions
- Better plan for the future

The insights gained from systematically measuring performance can be truly amazing. For example, one company had previously spent considerable time and effort measuring its production process, focusing especially on the related performance measures of cost, cycle time, and quality. Unfortunately, it had completely ignored the associated distribution process that accompanied the production process.

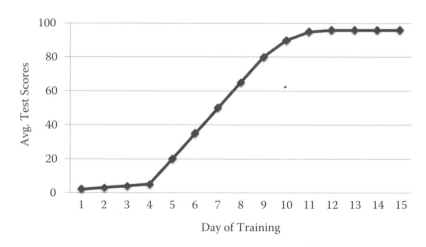

FIGURE 1.4
Average daily test scores.

Discovering this oversight, they finally began to put in place baseline and descriptive trending measures that could capture total enterprise performance, from initial production through distribution and final delivery. Distribution was defined as beginning when the product left the production line and ending when it was physically unloaded at the customer's receiving dock. Of great importance to the company, it was only at this final end point (representing actual customer receipt of the product) that the company was physically paid.

After the company began to measure the performance of the total enterprise, it was astounded at what it found. The production portion of total product cycle time measured only about 11%, which translated to approximately 2 weeks. Some 90% of total product cycle time (representing over 3 months) was tied up in distribution; that is, the company had a finished product that theoretically could be transformed into cash but it was spending an inexorable amount of time in an "unpaid" distribution pipeline. An inordinate amount of that distribution time was in various temporary storage sites within the company's own plant complex.

Finally understanding the problem, the company quickly took steps to shorten cycle time associated with distribution. It also established additional performance measures that would capture all aspects of the distribution process. The immediate result was an increase in cash flow because the company could now more quickly collect on its finished products. Looking back, one rather irritated top manager wanted to know why the situation had existed so long without being corrected. Although many excuses were made, in the end it simply reinforced that axiom that you cannot understand, improve, or manage what you do not quantitatively measure.

In essence, quantitatively measuring performance can help drive desired results at any level—be it at the organizational, departmental, individual, or process level. Such measures can also help identify problem areas and permit a better and deeper understanding of what truly drives performance within an organization. Before discussing performance measurement further, I will first define some important concepts.

> Quantitatively measuring performance can help drive desired business results.

KEY CONCEPTS AND DEFINITIONS

Some key concepts and definitions relating to performance measurement include:

- **Asymptote.** A straight line that is the limiting value of a curve; a performance barrier, limit, or wall.
- **Baseline performance.** This is the current level at which an organization, process, or function is performing. A company currently producing 25 units per week has a current baseline performance of 25 units per week.
- **Descriptive measure.** A type of performance measure that describes what is happening and has happened. Also referred to as a "lagging indicator."
- **Diagnostic measure.** A type of performance measure useful in determining why something is happening or has happened. Diagnostic measures can often provide insight into how to improve a performance-related problem.
- **Evaluation.** A judgment of worth or value that ideally should be based on some set of quantitative performance measures. Quantitatively measuring performance represents a critical means for making better evaluative judgments.
- **Family of measures.** This represents a group of usually four to six interrelated but still separate key aspects (or family members) of performance. A family of measures should constitute the key drivers or "oomph" factors that truly affect performance. Key types of measures within a family of measures typically include:
  - Productivity measures (e.g., 25 units produced per week)
  - Quality measures (e.g., call representatives had an overall customer service rating of 4.3 out of a 5-point scale)
  - Timeliness measures (e.g., 96% of all orders are delivered on time)
  - Cycle time measures (e.g., on average, it takes 78 minutes to perform a MRI at a hospital)
  - Resource utilization measures (e.g., a recently opened large training facility is currently being used only 43% of the time)
  - Cost measures (e.g., average publication costs currently average $7.63 per manual)

- **In-process performance measures.** This is often a "means" performance measure collected within a process. For example, if a process is comprised of three major activities, the cycle time and cost of each activity would be an example of an in-process measure. If the example is associated with some type of production process, so too would be the number of defects associated with each of the three activities.
- **Key performance factors.** These performance variables are especially critical in achieving a desired set of outcomes. Key performance factors are commonly linked to core products, services, and associated customer expectations. For example, in a service industry, timeliness, quality, and cost represent three key oomph factors that critically affect performance. Key performance factors should always be measured.
- **Measurement.** Involves ascertaining the size, amount, or degree of something. Measurements can be quantitative, which means that something is numerically expressible or actually "countable," or qualitative, which reflects more of a judgment or opinion of quality. Although qualitative measures can have much value, quantitative measures often provide more concrete and fact-based information.
- **Outcome measures.** Represent the "end" result of a process or activity, or what is actually "produced." If a maintenance department completes five preventive maintenance (PM) tasks in a day, the outcome measure would be "five completed PM tasks."
- **Performance.** An actual accomplishment, outcome, or result—or what is left at the end of the day after everyone has gone home. In this context performance should not be confused with work behavior. Performance focuses on an actual accomplishment or produced output. An example of a performance accomplishment is the ability to correctly process 50 medical insurance claims in a single day.
- **Performance goal.** This is a targeted level of accomplishment expressed as a tangible and measurable objective against which actual achievement is compared. For example, a performance goal may be to process, on average, 60 procurement requisitions per day. Performance goals are also sometimes called performance standards.
- **Performance index.** This is usually a number expressing some performance-related property or ratio. Performance indexes are particularly useful in ranking or comparing two or more entities.

- **Performance indicator.** This is a comparative performance metric used to answer the question, "How are we doing?" along a specific performance dimension and associated performance goal. The actual average number of procurement requisitions processed per day is an example of a performance indicator. If the performance goal is to process 60 requisitions per day and the procurement department is only processing on average 30 requisitions per day, then the answer to the "how are we doing" question is "not very well!" Note that performance indicators have little value unless they are compared to an associated performance goal or standard.

- **Performance measure.** Represents a numerical expression of how well something—be it a process, system, individual, etc.—is or has been doing (i.e., performing). Performance measures capture the extent to which a desired outcome or output is being achieved. However, to do so normally involves having a stated performance goal and associated set of performance metrics. In this regard, a performance measure and a performance indicator are essentially synonymous.

- **Performance measurement.** This is the process of measuring actual outcomes or the end goal of performance, as well as the means of achieving that outcome as represented by in-process measures.

- **Performance measurement hierarchy.** This is when the same performance measure (e.g., cycle time) is tailored to different user needs at different levels within an organization. For example, while frontline supervisors are probably most interested in the cycle time of their own particular activity, the general manager is more interested in the total cycle time of all combined activities from beginning to end.

- **Performance measurement system.** This is normally a graphical and numerical information system (often referred to as a performance dashboard or scorecard) used to monitor, assess, diagnose, and achieve desired performance levels. A performance measurement system involves defining, developing, collecting, synthesizing, delivering, and displaying performance-related information. Such systems should capture both outcome- and means (or in-process)-related performance information. All of the varying elements of an organization's performance measurement program comprise a performance measurement system. Note that to achieve maximum benefit, performance measurement systems must be directly tied to upstream key organizational performance drivers and, in turn, linked to downstream performance improvement efforts. Accordingly, key performance factors should always drive what to measure. In turn, derived measures should determine what and how to improve performance.

- **Performance metric.** This is a specific performance measure such as the number of days to manufacture a product. If we want to go on a diet and lose weight, then "pounds" would be our performance metric.

- **Predictive measure.** A type of performance measure that helps extrapolate what may happen (but has not yet happened) on the basis of what is happening and has happened. Also referred to as a "leading indicator."

- **Process.** This represents the transformation and blending of a set of inputs into a (hopefully) more valuable set of outputs. Outputs can be products, services, accomplished tasks, and even (improved) people. A process can be further divided into a series of interrelated activities that can be further subdivided into individual process steps. Approving and calculating insurance claims, producing a product, or providing healthcare all involve processes. As noted, a performance measurement system should measure the outcomes associated with a process and the means or in-process steps involved with achieving that outcome.

- **SMART measures.** An acronym referencing that performance measures should be Specific, Measurable, Actionable, Relevant, and Timely.

- **$y = f(x)$.** A common performance formula that states some outcome y is a function of variable set x. In this usage, y represents a performance accomplishment or the "end," while variable set x represents the "means" for achieving that end or outcome. Often and surprisingly, only a very small set of x values truly determine outcome y. It is this small set of x values that represent the key performance or real oomph factors that must be measured, along with associated y measures. In developing any performance measurement system then, it is always important to measure both the outcome (y) and the critical means for deriving that outcome (the x values).

SUMMARY

Increasingly, companies are transitioning from management by opinion to management by hard fact and concrete evidence. They are collecting real numbers and using those numbers to set, monitor, and achieve desired performance levels. A key enabler in this transition from opinion- to fact-based management is the development of a performance measurement system. The goal of any performance measurement system is to provide the right people with the right performance-related information at the right time to make the right (or at least better informed) decisions. However, collecting performance-related information that provides little to no value is a costly proposition that wastes scarce resources and should always be avoided. Accordingly, always collect only those measures that truly relate to those oh-so-important oomph factors that critically drive wanted (and sometimes even unwanted) performance outcomes.

2

Types of Performance Measures

Don't measure what you can't or won't use.

Most companies collect performance measures. Unfortunately, some of those companies rarely, if ever, actually use them. Instead, they create an attractive performance measure display panel on some obscure wall and then basically ignore the collected data altogether. The reality is that collecting performance measures takes real effort and time, and that effort and time cost real dollars. If collected performance measures are not going to be used and simply ignored, why collect them in the first place?

The key to any successful performance measurement effort is to collect only those performance measures that can and will actually be used, that is, to collect only those measures that can help each of us better understand, manage, and improve the performance of our respective organizations. In this case, "those measures" represent critical factors that truly drive performance.

The first step in any performance measurement development process is to determine what types of performance-related information are actually needed to better operate, manage, understand, and/or improve an organization, department, or process, that is, to complete the statement, "I need performance-related information in order to ..." For example, I need performance-related information in order to better track how long it takes to fill a customer order or how much it costs to mine a ton of ore. Knowing such needed performance-related information can help us better identify which measures to collect. It can also help us identify who the right people are to receive the collected information and when they need to receive it. Remember, the end goal of any performance measurement system is to translate collected "numbers" into actionable knowledge. Accordingly, we want to ensure that we are not providing the wrong information to the wrong people at the wrong time.

> The key to collecting performance measures is to identify those specific measures that will actually help drive desired results and that can be translated into actionable knowledge.

Performance measures can be used for several different purposes. Such purposes can range from determining current performance levels to predicting future ones to diagnosing a particular performance problem. However, regardless of the types of measures used, a good performance measurement system should always provide:

- Descriptive value: Describing what is happening and has happened
- Diagnostic value: Assisting us in better understanding why something is happening or has happened
- Predictive value: Helping us extrapolate what may happen (but has not yet happened) on the basis of what is happening and has happened

The following sections examine each of these general performance measurement categories in greater detail.

DESCRIPTIVE MEASURES

A descriptive measure describes *what is happening or has happened*. Such measures commonly depict specific outcomes and are often used to trend a particular phenomena over time. Accordingly, descriptive measures are also termed *lagging indicators*, indicating a predominantly backward or rearview-mirror view. Descriptive measures routinely include baseline and trending performance measures.

Baseline Performance Measures

Baseline measurements are some of the most important measures that can be gathered. They answer the question, "Where am I starting from?" Also called "as is" measures, baseline measures establish a baseline for current performance, forming the basis for all subsequent measures and associated improvement efforts. If we do not know where we are starting an improvement effort from, then it is virtually impossible to say that we have actually improved something 6 months later.

For example, the goal of going on a diet is to lose weight. Unless we know our starting weight, we cannot determine whether our diet is succeeding. Our initial starting weight represents our baseline "diet" measure. This baseline measure allows us to document future improvements, in this case represented by number of pounds (hopefully) lost. As illustrated in Figure 2.1, which displays the average cycle time of process X, a baseline measure is the first point on the graph. In this instance, it is 8 days.

Collecting initial baseline measures usually represents lots of work—especially for processes that have never been measured before—but these initial efforts are critical to the development and success of any performance measurement system or associated performance improvement effort. No baseline measures essentially means no performance measurement system, and you cannot improve what you do not measure. So always start with collecting baseline or "as is" measures, establishing a starting point to compare subsequent changes or improvements against.

> A baseline measure answers the question, "Where am I starting from?"

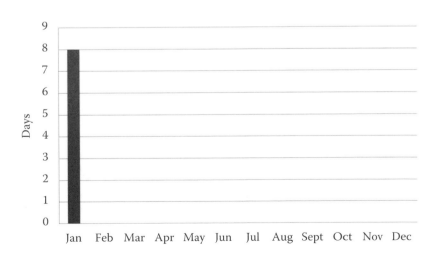

FIGURE 2.1
Initial baseline measurement.

Trending Performance Measures

A trending performance measure shows how something is doing over time by comparing something—usually an activity, outcome, output, or some other wanted or unwanted accomplishment—with a predetermined baseline measure. Figure 2.2 plots average processing cycle time over a 12-month period. It begins with an initial baseline measure of 8 days, as previously illustrated in Figure 2.1. It then tracks resultant changes over the next 12 months. As illustrated, average processing cycle time has decreased by about 50% over a 12-month period, a very wanted outcome.

Conversely, Figure 2.3 depicts an unwanted trend, here illustrated by an increase in the number of accidents as a function of time. Although trending performance measures cannot tell us why something may be happening (i.e., why an increase in the number of accidents is occurring), they can tell us what is and has been happening.

As such, trending measures can highlight accomplished performance levels over a specified time period. Comparing trending measures with an initial baseline measure quickly answers the question, "How are we doing?"

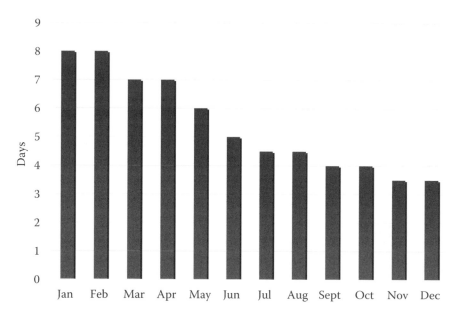

FIGURE 2.2
Trending performance measures.

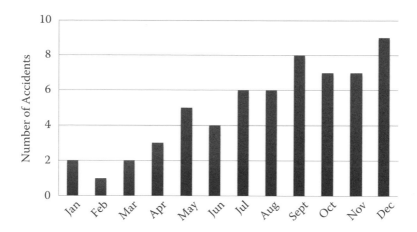

FIGURE 2.3
An unwanted safety performance-related trend.

In regards to Figure 2.2, the answer would be "quite well." Unfortunately, a more negative "not very well" answer would be given for Figure 2.3.

> Descriptive trending measures depict levels of performance as a function of time.

DIAGNOSTIC MEASURES

Frequently, specific performance problems are identified through performance measurement. Although you cannot improve what you do not measure, sometimes you also cannot even identify what is wrong unless you measure something. Unlike descriptive performance measures that tell us *what* is happening, diagnostic measures can help tell us *why* something is happening and even provide prescriptive advice on how to fix it. Diagnostic measures usually delve deeper into a system and often represent process, control, or other types of lower-level measures.

For example, two SWAT teams might complete a tactical shooting obstacle course in essentially the same time: team A in 64 seconds and team B in 63.5 seconds. From an outcome and descriptive point of view, the two teams' performances are essentially the same. Delving deeper, however, we see that although the outcome, here represented by overall course completion time as measured in seconds, is essentially the same, the performance at the individual stage and interstage levels comprising the obstacle course is decidedly different. This difference is illustrated in Figure 2.4. If our goal is to improve individual team performance, then on the basis of Figure 2.4 we would probably approach any improvement effort very differently for team A than we would for team B.

As illustrated in Figure 2.4, diagnostic measures can provide much greater and often more prescriptive information regarding a particular performance outcome. Such measures provide the "why" of performance.

Let's examine a more detailed example. In Figure 2.5, trending data indicate that average processing cycle time is suddenly and unexpectedly increasing, not continuing to decrease as expected. In such instances, the question "Why?" arises. This is usually followed by the question, "Where is the problem area?" Diagnostic measures can help provide that "where" answer. They attempt to orient you to a specific problem area. In many instances, and as illustrated here, trending performance measures can also serve as diagnostic measures.

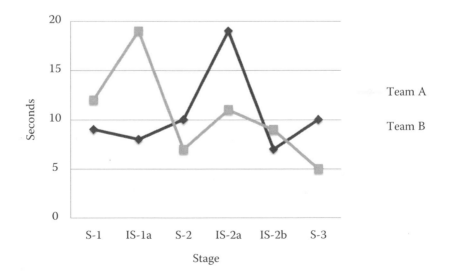

FIGURE 2.4
Diagnostic measures of team performance.

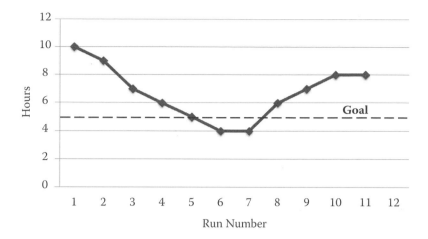

FIGURE 2.5
A process performance chart showing an increase in average cycle times.

Assume that the process illustrated in Figure 2.5 is composed of three major activities (1, 2, and 3). Also assume that cycle time data are collected for each of these three activities. The information in turn is combined to create the graph depicted in Figure 2.5. Examining each of these three activity-related cycle time graphs separately as illustrated in Figure 2.6 quickly identifies that the recent increase in cycle time is associated with activity 3. In this case, performance measures help us diagnose where the problem resides. Now instead of asking "What is causing cycle time to suddenly increase?" we can be more specific. We are able to ask, "What is causing cycle time to suddenly increase in activity 3?"

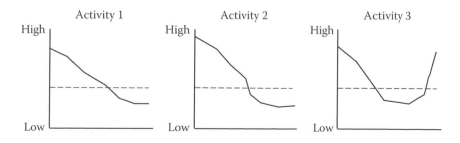

FIGURE 2.6
Activity-related cycle time graphs.

Additional time-related measures may be able to narrow the problem area down even further. For example, if average processing delay times are being trended for specific operations within activity 3, we may be able to determine that operation Y in particular is causing problems. Being able to access the performance-related information as illustrated in Figures 2.6 and 2.7, we can now be even more specific in our questioning. We are able to ask, "Why are processing delay times associated with operation Y in activity 3 suddenly increasing?" Armed with this kind of information, we can better focus subsequent corrective actions on the actual problem area.

Diagnostic measures can also sometimes help prevent a problem from occurring in the first place. For example, one call center carefully tracks the time it takes to respond to customer requests. At any time of the day, front-line supervisors can immediately access computer-generated data to view how customer requests are queuing up. They can instantly determine the amount of time that has elapsed on any given request. If an unacceptable backlog is beginning to accumulate, supervisors can quickly shift requests around to other workers. This computer-based performance tracking system greatly helps supervisors meet the company's self-imposed time deadlines regarding customer waiting times. It also helps ensure happy customers. As illustrated, diagnostic measures help us better understand why something is happening and identify potential problem areas.

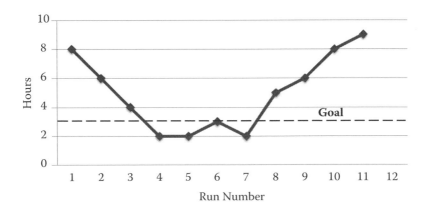

FIGURE 2.7
Average processing delay time chart for a specific operation within an activity.

> A diagnostic measure helps to better identify why something is happening and pinpoint specific problem areas.

Descriptive measures can also often be used as diagnostic measures and vice versa. A good example of such dual use is a control-type performance measure. A control measure (often in the form of a control chart) answers the question, "Am I staying within some predetermined boundary or tolerance?" Usually used as a rapid feedback system, control measures provide early warnings that something is starting to stray from a predetermined or required performance level.

For example, an organization may determine that six quality defects per production run is the maximum tolerable number of defects acceptable. The control chart illustrated in Figure 2.8 would alert managers to a potential problem if defect rates should suddenly increase beyond this allowable control limit. Control charts such as Figure 2.8 not only describe what is happening but can also pinpoint a specific "where it is happening" problem very rapidly.

If it is important to keep a process within predetermined levels, then you need control-type performance measures. As described in Chapter 6, control performance measures must often be collected in near real time. This information in turn must be provided immediately to the people directly performing or managing the particular function or process. Control measures unfortunately are of little value or use after the fact.

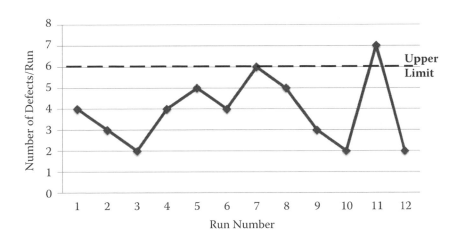

FIGURE 2.8
A typical control chart.

PREDICTIVE MEASURES

Predictive measures are used to infer into the future or extrapolate from one performance measure in one setting or environment to another. They attempt to predict what *may* happen but to date has not happened. Such predictive "what may happen" interpretations are often predicated or based on "what has already happened" descriptive measures. Accordingly, predictive measures are also sometimes termed *leading indicators*, suggesting that they represent forward-looking types of measures.

In truth and despite rhetoric to the contrary, good predictive measures are sometimes difficult to develop and almost always require some type of extrapolation and interpretation. Figure 2.9a depicts monthly sales of a relatively new product line. Conversely, Figure 2.9b graphs monthly sales of a fairly mature product line.

If one had to predict sales levels of the two product lines, obviously the task would be much easier for the product line depicted in Figure 2.9b than the one depicted in Figure 2.9a. Accordingly, mature systems (or stable systems under good control) with abundant performance data are much easier to predict than are immature systems with little historical performance data or that constitute highly variable systems.

For example, if we know that a manufacturing system can reliably produce 10 units of something each week, then we can fairly accurately predict and plan that approximately 500 units will be produced each year (assuming time off for holidays, etc.). However, if our manufacturing system is unstable, one week producing 2 units and the next week producing 12 units, then making such future planning predictions becomes a much harder task.

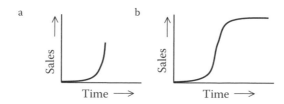

FIGURE 2.9
A depiction of sales levels for a (a) new and (b) mature product line.

Sometimes with a bit of extra work we can determine the "reliability" and associated predictability of a system. Imagine, for example, that you are the general manager of a Major League Baseball team and are desperately in need of a solid and reliably hitting third baseman. You have compiled a short list of five players (A–E) all having roughly similar batting averages. Additionally, they all seem to handle the ball about the same. Which one do you pick?

Let's assume that we have 5 years of batting history for each player. To measure the reliability and predictability of the "batting system," we can calculate a standard deviation for each player on the basis of those 5 years of batting averages. Remember, a standard deviation measures the spread or variance about an average or mean.

Performing this additional step indicates that many of the players have high standard deviations, indicating some really good years interspersed with some really lousy years. Player C, however, has an amazingly low standard deviation, indicating that he seems to perform at a very consistent level year after year; in other words, he is a very reliable batter. Although the general manager cannot guarantee that player C will perform at this level if he acquires him, there is a very high level of "predictability" that he will continue to perform in the future in the same way that he has performed in the past. Accordingly, the general manager decides to go with player C.

Predictive measures thus help us to extrapolate into the future. Often, but certainly not always, the best predictors of future performance are past and present performance. In such instances, using descriptive measures to describe what is happening and has happened can better help us predict what may happen.

> Predictive measures extrapolate into the future, allowing us to determine what may happen but to date has not happened.

SUMMARY

Performance measures can be used for several different purposes and can answer varying types of performance-related questions. Regardless of the types of measures used, a good performance measurement system should always provide:

- Descriptive value: Describing what is happening and has happened
- Diagnostic value: Assisting us in better understanding why something is or has happened
- Predictive value: Helping us to infer what may happen (but to date has not happened)

Such descriptive, diagnostic, and predictive measures are not mutually exclusive. A descriptive measure can also be used as a diagnostic measure, describing not only what is happening, but also why something may be happening. The same "what is happening" descriptive measures can also sometimes help predict what may happen.

Regardless of the types of performance measures used, such measures should always help us better understand, manage, and improve the performance levels of our respective organizations. By initially assessing what performance-related information needs to exist, as well as better understanding how such information can and will be used, a performance measurement system can be better designed, implemented, and maintained.

Creating a performance measurement system

Step 1. Define needed types of performance-related information that can help achieve desired performance levels.

3

A Family of Measures

Measure the critical few, not the trivial many.

Every organization wants to achieve the highest levels of performance possible. Yet to do so almost always requires a delicate balancing act of some critical set of variables that affect performance. For example, few if any companies can afford to focus solely on quality while completely ignoring cost, productivity, cycle time, and the safety of their operations. Instead, they must divide their efforts among these critical performance factors so that optimum—but not necessarily maximum and equal—effort is spent on each.

For example, we might think that manufacturing companies only have to make (and distribute) stuff. But in actuality, they must creatively *design*, efficiently *make*, and successfully *sell* stuff, all within an appropriate cost structure that provides an acceptable margin of profit. Other organizations have to do the same thing.

A nongovernment organization (NGO) involved in clearing landmines and unexploded ordnance must balance productivity (as measured by amount of land cleared), quality (represented by how "thoroughly" the land is cleared), and safety. A service-related company must focus on the quality of its service, response time (or how quickly it can respond to customer needs), and cost. An offshore oil well drilling company needs to focus on productivity (as measured by daily footage drilled), cost, logistics, and safety. Because all organizations must work with several key performance variables, a single measure of performance is rarely adequate. Rather, a family of measures is required.

> Organizations must attempt to successfully optimize a key set of performance variables.

Think for a moment about your car's dashboard. Grouped in front of you is a series of measures that represent key performance factors related to the task of driving a car. Usually there are about six performance measure displays: a speedometer, odometer, tachometer, temperature gauge, fuel gauge, and oil pressure gauge (additionally there are various "idiot lights" that come on if something goes wrong). You really need each of these, not just one. Although only having a speedometer may help keep you from getting a speeding ticket, it will not prevent you from running out of gas. Nor will it let you know that your engine is overheating or how far you have traveled. The various measures represented on your dashboard, although interrelated to the task of driving, still provide separate types of required information.

We could certainly add many more driving-related measures, and many newer cars have. In fact, we could easily place gauges everywhere. This would provide an array of performance-related information. For example, we could have a gauge showing the number of "dings" in the car's body. Or we could add a gauge indicating that both bumpers are still firmly intact. The list could be almost endless. However, viewing such a cumbersome array, could we as drivers easily identify what is important to the core task of driving a car—the critical few?

Many companies take the same approach in developing a performance measurement system. They try to measure everything and in the process they dilute what is really important. For example, one major company found itself collecting more than 100 different performance measures. Yet it found that it was actually using only a few of them. Realizing the error, the company completely scrapped its existing performance measurement system. It now collects only a handful of critical measures, focusing on the critical few instead of the trivial many. These critical few measures represent what is commonly termed a *family of measures*.

The concept of a family of measures is normally associated with the excellent work of Carl G. Thor (see Christopher and Thor in Further Reading). As noted in Chapter 1, a family of measures usually represents four to six interrelated but still separate key aspects of performance. A family of measures captures key activities and outputs of critical importance to an organization—the real oomph factors. Such measures are normally linked to core products and services, customer expectations, enabling processes, or an organization's critical performance objectives.

Ideally, a family of measures measure the critical "*x*" factors, or the key drivers of some wanted (and even unwanted) performance outcome; remember our $y = f(x)$ or "outcome y is a function of variable set x" formula. For example, if we are interested in creating a family of measures for life expectancy, we would first want to identify the key determinants that affect how long we live. It turns out that there are really only three key factors as measured by infant mortality rates, adolescent mortality rates, and maternal mortality rates. Our family of measures would thus consist of these various mortality rate measures.

Ideally a short scan of a family of measures can quickly and concisely provide anyone with a good overview of how well an organization is performing. A family of measures basically serves as a performance snapshot in time, succinctly capturing the critical few.

KEY CHARACTERISTICS

The following sections describe characteristics that any family of measures should possess.

Accurately Measure Key Performance Variables

A family of measures typically incorporates the following types of measures:

- Productivity: This is usually expressed as the relationship between the physical inputs and outputs of a defined process, that is, the relationship between the number of outputs versus the resources consumed in producing those outputs. Frequently a productivity measure answers the question "How much?" or "How many?" by whom or what. An example of a productivity measure is 55 units produced by a four-person crew in 1 week, or in a mining example tons produced per day. In logistics, productivity is often measured by tons of material transported per day or per mile.
- Quality: This performance measure commonly includes both internal measurements like scrap, number of rejects, and defects per unit, as well as external customer satisfaction ratings or customer repeat frequencies.

- Timeliness: This pertains to things like percentage of on-time deliveries or percentage of orders shipped when promised. Basically, timeliness measures assess whether you are doing what you say you are going to do when you say you will do it.

- Cycle time: This measure refers to the amount of time it takes to proceed from one defined point in a process to another. A cycle time measurement measures how long something takes. For example, a typical cycle time measurement may be the amount of time on average it takes from when a customer places an order to when the customer actually receives the order.

- Resource utilization: This is a measurement of resources used versus resources available for use. Resource utilization can apply to such things as machines, vehicles, facilities, and even people. A labor resource utilization of 40% indicates that personnel are being productively utilized only 40% of the time they are available for work. Sometimes something can be overutilized as well. By calculating utilization rates, an organization often finds that it does not really need more resources. Instead, it just needs to better utilize the resources it already has.

- Cost: This measure is especially useful if calculated on a per-unit basis. For example, one training program costs $50,000 to deliver and another program costs $25,000. Which one is more expensive? Using the unit of *cost per student training day* reveals that the $25,000 course is almost twice as expensive as the $50,000 course. In some instances, although organizations may have a great deal of information on total costs, they actually have very little per-unit cost data.

- Safety: Often companies must carefully balance productivity and safety. Measures of accident rates per so many labor hours, near misses, etc., can quantify how well an organization is doing on the safety front.

Depending on the particular setting, there are certainly other types of performance-related measurements that can be included in a family of measures. Perhaps the best advice is to always measure what is important and use these measures to help achieve desired performance levels.

> Measure what is important, using what is measured to help achieve desired performance levels.

As previously noted, in some instances a company may develop multiple metrics associated within a single "family of measures" member. For example, one highly successful service company focuses on rapidly responding to its customers. Indeed, the company has discovered, as have many other service companies, that customer response time is a critical success factor in maintaining continued customer loyalty. Fortunately, the company currently has a very loyal customer base. Unfortunately, such premium customers demand good service and they demand it immediately. As a consequence, the company has developed a very time-oriented set of performance measures, many of them relating to speed of response in dealing with customer needs and requests.

Include a Comparative Basis to Assist in Better Understanding Displayed Performance Levels

Examine Figure 3.1 carefully. Then try to answer the question, "How well is this aspect of the process performing?" Basically you cannot, because you have nothing to compare the numbers with. For instance, a speedometer that reads 50 mph cannot tell you whether you are going too fast,

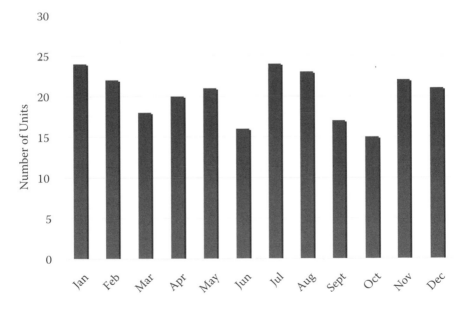

FIGURE 3.1
A production graph with no embedded comparative information.

too slow, or just right unless you also know the posted speed limit for the road you are traveling on.

It is important when developing a family of measures to also have a means of bringing meaning to the measurements. Remember, a performance measure should always have an associated performance goal or standard—a targeted level of accomplishment expressed as a tangible and measurable objective against which actual achievement is compared. For example, the only way we know that we really have a fever is because we first know what a "normal" temperature is (98.6°F) and can compare our current temperature (101°F) with that normal figure.

Figure 3.2 illustrates the same graph presented in Figure 3.1. However, Figure 3.2 now includes a production goal represented by a dashed line that quickly and clearly indicates that production levels are consistently falling short of the desired goal set by the company. In this example, the company is either experiencing a serious and continuing production problem or has set a very unrealistic and unachievable goal for itself.

Be Collected and Distributed on a Timely Basis

This topic is discussed in more detail in Chapter 6, but basically, to be usable performance measurement collection and distribution/display frequencies must be driven by user needs. For example, it would not do much good to have your car's speedometer only "come on" for 5 seconds out of

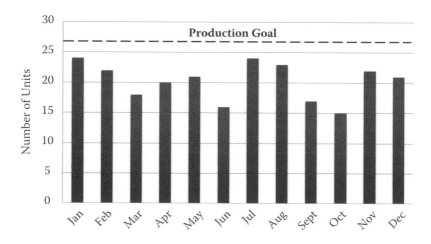

FIGURE 3.2
A production graph including embedded comparative information.

every 5 minutes. While driving, you must be able to monitor your speed almost continuously, that is, you must have a performance measurement display system that is constantly "displaying."

Increasingly, as business transactions speed up and customer needs and market conditions often seem to change overnight (if not quicker), performance measures must be collected and displayed at the same near real-time frequency. However, this near real-time need can place severe demands on any performance measurement collection and distribution system. In this regard, advances in computer-based, automated performance measurement systems hold much promise.

Be Analyzable on a Macro and Micro Basis

As noted in Chapter 2, performance measures can be used for many different purposes. Frequently, in-depth and more detailed information about a specific measure and bigger picture overviews are needed. In this regard, any performance measurement system should be like a zoom lens on a camera, providing both "big picture" wide-angle views as well as increasingly close-up views that provide greater in-depth knowledge and associated granularity.

Creating a hierarchy of the same family of measures allows one to "roll up" lower levels of information to ever-higher levels. Such family-of-measure hierarchies also provide a means to "drill down," providing lower levels of detail as well. Performance measurement hierarchies are described in more detail in Chapter 4.

Cannot Be Easily Manipulated to Achieve Desired Results

In selecting a family of performance measures, make sure that they cannot be easily manipulated by someone to achieve desired results. Selecting measures that are true indicators of core performance will usually prevent such "creative" accounting systems. Performance measures often influence human behavior. Just make sure that they are influencing the right types of behavior.

For example, one company launched a plant-wide process improvement effort. Top management decided to carefully track the number of performance teams chartered within each division and the number of meetings each team held. They thought these traits represented good performance indicators for what they called division commitment. However, no measures of actual accomplishment were ever instituted. As such, some crafty division managers simply launched lots of teams and had them meet frequently, but only for very short periods of time. Unfortunately, nothing of substance was ever accomplished in any of the team meetings, yet the associated performance measures of number of teams launched and frequency of meetings held looked great to unsuspecting and naive top management.

The very process of developing a family of performance measures will often help a company focus on what is actually needed to be successful—those oh-so-important oomph factors. Although measuring everything might seem nice, such efforts frequently dilute an organization's ability to focus on what is really important. Therefore, measure only what is really important and what real people will use.

> Creating a family of performance measures will often help an organization focus on what is truly important.

CORRELATED MEASURES

As discussed in Chapter 2, collecting performance measures takes real effort and time, which costs any organization real dollars. Therefore, it is important to collect only those measures that provide the greatest information and are most usable. In some instances two (or more) performance measures may be very closely related or correlated with each other. In such instances, it makes little sense to collect both measures in a family of measures. Instead, simply collect one measure (usually the easiest one) and extrapolate the collected information to the other measure if needed.

Correlation refers to the degree of relatedness between two (or more) variables. Performance measures can be either positively or negatively correlated. A positive correlation means that as one variable increases or decreases, another variable also increases or decreases in the same fashion. A negative correlation describes two variables that are inversely related: as one increases, the other decreases. Correlations can range from 0 (essentially no correlation) to 1.0 (a perfect correlation).

Figure 3.3 plots team salaries versus regular season team wins for the 2008 Major League Baseball season. The calculated correlation is 0.33—a

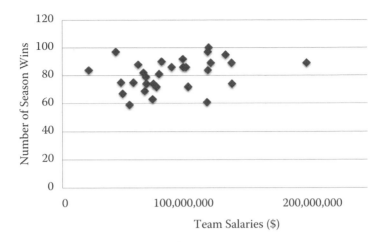

FIGURE 3.3
A relatively low (0.33) correlation plot.

moderately low correlation. From such plots we can conclude that the amount of money spent on team salaries is not as significant as many owners might think and does not correlate or drive the number of regular season team wins. Conversely, Figure 3.4 plots accuracy versus time in a tactical shooting competition. Here we see a very strong correlation (0.89), indicating that shooting accuracy is a very strong determinant of final course time.

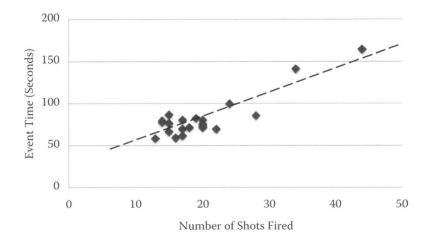

FIGURE 3.4
A fairly high (0.89) correlation plot.

Cycle time and labor costs are good examples of two performance measures that are often correlated. For example, if you are collecting cycle time data and cycle time is essentially composed of labor hours, then you only need hourly labor rates to calculate actual labor costs; that is, one performance measure, in this instance cycle time, can give you a second measure—cost—without going to the effort of directly collecting cost data.

It is essential when developing a family of measures to make sure that two or more of the measures are not directly correlated to each other. If they are, collect only one performance measure and simply extrapolate to the other measure as needed. A family of measures should always contain separate measures that are not closely correlated.

> A family of measures represent interrelated but still separate key aspects of performance.

SOME REPRESENTATIVE EXAMPLES OF A FAMILY OF MEASURES

Every organization is somewhat unique. Therefore, an organization's specific family of performance measures should reflect this uniqueness. They should be custom-fitted to the organization's particular needs and to those critical factors that truly drive performance within the organization. As noted, a family of measures typically involves general types of individual measures:

- Productivity
- Quality
- Timeliness
- Cycle time
- Resource utilization
- Cost
- Safety

Some specific examples of measures that might be included in a family of measures from different business and industrial sectors are:

- Accounting-related performance measures
  - Number of errors reported by outside auditors

- Payroll processing cycle time
- Billing (preparation and sending) cycle time
- Credit application approval cycle time
- Average number of days from payment receipt to processing

- Customer-service-related performance measures
  - Average cycle time to process customer request or service order
  - Average time for customer to speak to a sales representative
  - Average order queue times
  - Customer repeat frequency
  - Number of customer-service-related complaints

- Engineering-related performance measures
  - Number of design change notices per engineering project
  - Engineer labor utilization
  - Number of drawing errors per design sheet
  - Percentage of total design time used for redesign
  - Percentage of on-time drawing release

- Extractive (oil, mining, etc.)-related performance measures
  - Average tons produced per shift
  - Average cost per ton
  - Average ore grade per ton
  - Average footage drilled per day
  - Average cost per foot drilled
  - Average rig setup time prior to drilling

- Healthcare-related performance measures (relating to operating theaters only)
  - Average cycle time of operating theater turnaround and/or changeover
  - Cost of materials per operation
  - Machine/instrument reliability and availability
  - Operating theater utilization rates
  - Delay time due to unavailable resources (e.g., personnel, equipment, or supplies)
  - Patient waiting times prior to surgery

- Information systems-related performance measures
  - Mean time between system interruptions
  - Mean time between unplanned system repairs
  - Mean time of planned system repairs
  - Number of help desk calls

- – Average response time to help desk complaints
- – Average time to resolve help desk complaints
- Mail-order-service-related performance measures
  - – Percentage of orders shipped when promised
  - – Average cycle time of customer order to customer receipt
  - – Percentage of orders returned because of service errors
  - – Percentage of total orders backordered
  - – Customer satisfaction ratings
- Maintenance-related performance measures
  - – Backlog of preventative maintenance tasks
  - – Percentage of maintenance-related downtime
  - – Call-back frequency for defective maintenance repairs
  - – Percentage of on-time maintenance service commitments
  - – Work order cycle time
  - – Average cycle time of preventative maintenance calls
- Manufacturing-related performance measures
  - – Number of defects per produced unit
  - – Per-unit cycle time and associated costs
  - – Labor/machine utilization
  - – Percentage of on-time production deliveries
  - – Percentage of manufacturing facility downtime
  - – Changeover cycle times
- Procurement/purchasing-related performance measures
  - – Percentage of supplies delivered per needed scheduled
  - – Purchase order cycle time
  - – Percentages of purchase orders returned because of errors
  - – Number of backordered items
- Sales-related performance measures
  - – Percentage of return sales
  - – Sales per day/week/month
  - – Sales per salesperson
  - – Average sales per number of sales calls
  - – Sales per sales unit (store, etc.)
- Shipping/trucking-related performance measures
  - – Total tonnage hauled per road mile
  - – Percentage of total road miles hauling empty
  - – Percentage of on-time pickups and deliveries
  - – Average length of cargo delays at distribution centers
  - – Accidents per 100,000 road miles

- – Tickets per 100,000 road miles
- – Number of breakdowns per 100,000 road miles
- Training-related performance measures
  - – Courses delivered per year
  - – Training facility utilization rate
  - – Cost per student training day
  - – Average pre–/post–test score improvement
  - – Number of development hours per one hour of instruction

The previous examples are by no means intended to represent an exclusive list. The key in creating a family of performance measures is to identify those measures that will actually help someone better understand, manage, control, and improve some aspect of his or her own work or that of the organization in general. It is also important to stress that when it comes to creating a family of measures, more is not always better. Remember, only measure the critical few, not the trivial many.

For example, one company collected some 24 different performance measures on a daily or weekly basis. Over time, the company had established a rather elaborate and costly performance measurement system, headed up by a single department. The company would proudly parade visitors past its performance indicator display boards, positioned strategically throughout the plant, and boast of their value and the fact that the company had won a *Best in Class* award for its performance measurement efforts. Anyone seeing the elaborate, color-coded displays could not help but be impressed. To the outside visitor, the company seemed to have an exemplary performance measurement program in place.

Eventually, however, someone within the company asked the question, "How is each performance measure actually being used and by whom?" The intent of the mini-audit was to show the value of each performance measure and how it was specifically being used to support day-to-day operations at the plant.

Surprisingly, and of some embarrassment to the company, only 4 of the 24 performance measures were actually being used. Interviewed workers, supervisors, and managers would say things like, "We live by these four performance measures. I could not do my job without them. But in all honesty, I do not even look at the others. They have no real value to me." However, they would always hastily add, "I am sure someone certainly uses them." Unfortunately and despite much effort, the company never could find the "someone" who used them.

Additional comments from the intended users indicated that two other measures that were not being collected, cycle time and machine utilization rates, would be very beneficial, adding a great deal of value to day-to-day activities. Realizing that an "unused more" is not always better when it comes to performance measurement, the company created a new family of measures consisting of the four measures that were already being used and the two new ones suggested by employees. Although the new family of measures meant less work for the department tasked with collecting and displaying performance-related information at the plant, it by no means diminished its value. Indeed, the value of the group actually increased.

SUMMARY

In an attempt to focus on the critical few and not the trivial many, some organizations use a family of performance measures. A family of measures usually represents four to six interrelated but separate key aspects of performance, representing the real drivers or oomph factors of performance. A family of measures captures key activities and outputs of critical importance to an organization. As such, they should be directly linked to core products and services, customer expectations, or an organization's primary mission and associated enabling objectives. Normally, a family of measures involves the following types of measures: productivity, quality, timeliness, cycle time, resource utilization, safety, and cost. In many instances, multiple measures of the same family member are collected, often at different levels within the organization.

Creating a performance measurement system

Step 1. Define needed types of performance-related information that can help achieve desired performance levels.
Step 2. Develop a relevant and usable family of measures.

4

Performance Measurement Hierarchies

> Provide the right level of performance-related information to the right people.

In Chapter 3, it was noted that a single measure rarely if ever captures all aspects of performance. Instead, the use of a family of measures was suggested. A family of measures commonly represents four to six interrelated but separate key aspects of performance.

Just as no single measure can adequately capture all aspects of performance, rarely can a single level of a specific measure be used throughout an organization. As illustrated in Figure 4.1, specific information needs relating to a particular performance measure span the gamut from the individual worker to the corporation. However, performance information needed by an individual to do his or her specific job is often very different from the information needed to manage at the department level, and the performance information needed to manage a factory or store is decidedly

FIGURE 4.1
Performance measurement needs differ based on organizational level.

different from information needed to manage the whole corporation. Although everyone might need quality or cycle time-related information, they need it at different levels. Therefore, a *performance measurement hierarchy* of the same family of measures member is often created.

Performance measurement hierarchies measure a similar aspect of performance, such as cycle time, but at different levels within the same organization. For example, a general manager usually requires different levels of performance-related information than do front-line supervisors or department managers. Commonly, as one goes "up" in a developed performance measurement hierarchy, descriptive and especially predictive or "leading indicator-type" measures become more important. This is because planning and strategic types of activities normally take place at these higher levels within an organization.

Conversely, at lower levels within an organization, descriptive and especially diagnostic measures are often more important. These lower levels within an organization represent where most day-to-day work operations take place. Accordingly, at these lower organizational levels real-time, "how are we doing now" information is often especially critical. Also, if a problem arises, front-line supervisors need diagnostic "what is wrong and where" performance information to take immediate corrective action.

Most organizations require a hierarchy of the same measure, measuring a similar aspect of performance but at different levels. Think of the example of turnaround time for a large jetliner at a major airport, something that almost all of us have personally experienced and observed. One key measure of this process is "gate" cycle time, here defined as the time between an aircraft arriving at a gate and leaving the gate. Speed and timeliness are critical performance factors in the airline industry and often determine whether an on-time "push back" occurs or not. Indeed, getting planes in and out of airports as fast and safely as possible helps ensure that tight schedules are maintained in an efficient manner.

Upon closer examination, the jet turnaround process may be divided into a series of activities, as depicted in Figure 4.2. Some of the activities are directly related. For example, arriving baggage must be unloaded before departing baggage can be loaded. The same is true with passengers. However, other activities are unrelated and independent of each other. For example, flight crews must complete their own set of steps and activities irrespective of passenger and baggage unloading and loading. General service and maintenance crews must also perform their own specific set

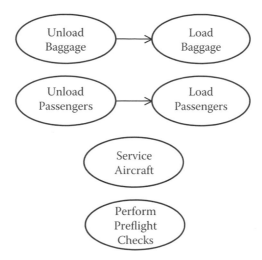

FIGURE 4.2
Jet turnaround process activities.

of activities, irrespective of the work that others are performing around them.

As such, the process consists of a whole—turning the jet around for departure. It also consists of a series of separate but interrelated activities (e.g., unloading and loading baggage). Yet in the end, all of these separate but interrelated activities must be completed before the whole can be accomplished or before the jet can actually push back from the terminal. If one activity is delayed, then the whole is delayed and frustrated and anxious passengers get to sit on the plane past their scheduled departure time.

Using the jet turnaround process and the performance measures of cycle time as an example, no single cycle time measure is universally applicable or relevant to everyone. Although the total jet turnaround cycle time may be of great significance to the general manager of flight operations, it does not have the same relevance to the manager of baggage handling nor does it have the same meaning to the person overseeing general servicing (including fueling) of the aircraft; that is, total turnaround cycle time is not a specific enough measure for these two individual subprocess owners.

The baggage manager wants to know how long it takes to get baggage on and off the plane. The person overseeing general service wants to know how long fueling and other service-related activities take. To better perform their jobs, they require more specific and relevant cycle time measures than just total turnaround cycle time—they need greater detail. Although the performance measure is still the same—that of cycle time— the required level of information varies from activity to activity and from individual to individual.

Additionally, if an airline company measures only total turnaround times and not lower-level component measures comprising that upper-level measure, and if all of a sudden they begin experiencing an unwanted increase in turnaround times, then they would have no means of identifying the specific problem area. Is it baggage, passenger, flight crew, or service turnaround times that are causing the problem? In this example, collecting information at lower activity levels not only answers the "how are we doing" question, but it can also help pinpoint problem areas if the answer is "not very well."

Tailoring performance measures to individual needs and differing levels of need is sometimes called making performance measures SMART (specific, measurable, actionable, relevant, and timely). The development of a performance measurement hierarchy makes measures more specific and relevant to a particular individual or organizational element. Hierarchies can help answer the question, "Who needs what level of performance-related information where and when?"

The pyramid-type chart shown in Figure 4.3 illustrates a performance measurement hierarchy in which lower-level measures are combined to create higher-level measures. As illustrated, higher-level measures are composed of two or more lower-level measures. At each higher level, more and more performance information is being aggregated into a single measure.

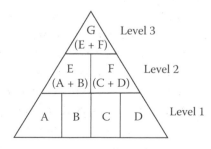

FIGURE 4.3
A performance measurement hierarchy.

In this example, a process is decomposed into three levels (1–3). Individual level 1 activities—comprised of activities A, B, C, and D—are combined into two higher subprocess levels designated E and F. In turn, subprocesses E and F representing level 2 measures are combined into a much higher aggregated level 3 measure, here represented by process G.

Studying Figure 4.3 can provide descriptive information as well as diagnostic information. If process measure G is within some predetermined and acceptable performance boundary, then a higher-level manager may not wish to study associated lower-level measures any further (e.g., level 1 and 2 measures). However, if process measure G is outside of an expected norm, then the manager can quickly delve deeper in the hierarchy for additional information. As illustrated, a well-constructed performance measurement hierarchy provides someone with both a "big picture" top view, as well as more specific and detailed lower-level views. This "drill-down" and greater granularity capability represents an especially positive performance measurement hierarchy-related feature.

ADVANTAGES

Creating a hierarchy of the same performance measure has several advantages, including:

- Providing specific and relevant performance-related information to different levels within an organization so that the right people can more easily access the right level of information at the right time. This "right stuff" makes the information more relevant, specific, meaningful, and usable. Once a performance measurement hierarchy is developed, it is fairly straightforward to answer the question, "Who gets what information when?"
- Collecting lower-level measures can be easily combined and "rolled up" into higher-level measures; therefore, higher-level measures do not have to be directly collected. Instead, they can be simply aggregated from previously collected lower-level measures (e.g., measure E = previously collected measure A + measure B).
- A performance measurement hierarchy also represents an excellent diagnostic system. Because higher-level measures can be easily decomposed into lower-level measures, such measures often provide

an effective means of zooming in on a performance-related problem. For example, if overall process defect rates go up, decomposing defect rates at the subprocess and activity level can assist in identifying where the unwanted increase is actually coming from.

A WORD OF CAUTION

When creating a performance measurement hierarchy, make sure that associated gaps between separate measures do not exist. For example, preventive maintenance of a large piece of equipment may consist of three major activities: cleaning (activity A), calibration (activity B), and testing and certification (activity C). The three activities also occur in a linear fashion, with cleaning occurring before calibration, and calibration occurring before testing and certification. Furthermore, each activity represents the efforts of a separate department. Let's further assume that each department measures cycle time from when the piece of equipment is received to when it is shipped to the next department. In this case, individual activity cycle time equals exit time minus entrance time (within a single department).

Using the two-level performance hierarchy concept illustrated in Figure 4.4, total process cycle time equals the combined cycle times of activities A (cleaning) + B (calibration) + C (testing and calibration). Unfortunately, that is in error because shipping or transportation time

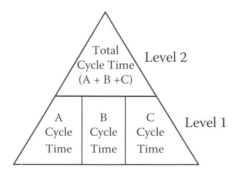

FIGURE 4.4
A performance measurement hierarchy comprised of two levels.

between activities A and B and between activities B and C are missing and are not being captured and added to total cycle time.

In this example, an accurate level 2 cycle time measure equals the sum of the individual cycle times of activities A, B, and C, plus transport times between activities A and B and between activities B and C. When creating a performance measurement hierarchy, always make sure that such missing gaps are not left out when aggregating upward to a higher-level measure.

One way to eliminate this common pitfall is to develop performance measures that are process aligned instead of functionally or departmentally aligned. In adopting a process view, all process elements, including in-between transport steps, are more easily captured and aggregated. As such, always try to avoid creating lower-level performance measures with associated missing gaps.

PERFORMANCE INDEXES

Recently, some organizations are translating performance measurement hierarchies into *performance indexes*. An index represents a number (or sometimes a formula) expressing some property or ratio of something, such as a price index. For example, the United Nations has developed a composite index called the Human Development Index (HDI). It is a summary measure of human development and is used to quantitatively compare one country to another. The HDI is composed of three underlying factors and associated measures: (1) *a long and healthy life*, as measured by life expectancy; (2) *knowledge*, as measured by adult literacy; and (3) *a decent standard of living*, as measured by per capita gross domestic product. In turn, each underlying factor is composed of its own aggregated components. Life expectancy, as noted earlier, is composed of infant-, adolescent-, and maternal-mortality rates.

> A performance index is a number expressing some performance-related property or ratio.

Let's develop a simple performance index using a sports-related example. You might be interested in creating an index of the shooting capability of professional basketball players on the basis of percentage of shots made. In basketball, players can make free throws worth one point each, lay-ups and jump shots worth two points each, and longer shots worth three points each. In each category, percentages can range from 0 to 100%. For example, player X might make 90% of his free throws or one-point shots, 45% of his two-point shots, and 30% of his longer three-point shots.

If each one-, two-, and three-point category is treated equally, then we could simply take one-third of the percentage of one-point shots plus one-third of the percentage of two-point shots, plus one-third of the percentage of three-point shots to create a shooting percentage index, or SPI. For player X, this would equal $(1/3 \times 0.9) + (1/3 \times 0.45) + (1/3 \times 0.3)$, or a SPI of 0.55.

The astute reader might ask why a one-point shot is treated the same as a two- or three-point shot. This does not seem quite fair! To provide greater "equity" among the different types of shots, we could normalize our developed performance index around two-point conversions. A one-point shot is now only half as important as a two-point shot, while a three-point shot is half again as important as a two-point shot. If we accept this "equalizing" logic, then we would have to multiply one-point shot percentages by 0.5 and three-point shot percentages by 1.5. The new formula for player X is now: $1/3(0.5 \times 0.9) + 1/3(0.45) + 1/3(1.5 \times 0.3)$, or a SPI of 0.45.

Such developed performance indexes provide a quick means to compare two or more related numbers. For example, if player X has a SPI of 0.45, player Y of 0.50, and player Z of 0.40, then it is a simple exercise to rank the players, with player Y having the best overall SPI followed by players X and Z. However, the only problem with such SPI-related rankings and performance indexes in general is that they do not by themselves provide any embedded lower-level information.

For example, player Y may actually be a great three-point shooter (thus elevating his SPI), but only a mediocre two-point shooter when compared to players X and Z. Unfortunately, this more detailed information is not readily discernible from a SPI figure alone. Often the real power of both performance indexes and performance measurement hierarchies comes from knowing the details, or the exact embedded numbers used to aggregate "up" to a higher level or summed index figure.

Depending on the circumstances and envisioned use, a performance index may have a great deal of applicability and utility, especially when providing big-picture comparative analyses between and among differing entities. However, as noted, a single performance index lacks the more detailed underlying information that is commonly found in aggregated and displayed performance measurement hierarchies. Yet depending on how performance indexes are developed and displayed, these underlying data can be readily incorporated, allowing the same type of drill-down capability in a performance index as found in a performance measurement hierarchy.

SUMMARY

Providing the right level of performance-related information to the right person(s) at the right time is critical for optimizing performance in any organization. In most instances, a hierarchy of differing levels of the same performance measure is required. The creation of a performance measurement hierarchy helps ensure that relevant and meaningful performance-related information is collected and distributed to the right levels within an organization.

A performance measurement hierarchy allows an organization to both aggregate performance information "up" through an organization, as well as "down" to individual departments and workers. Performance measurement hierarchies can also be easily translated into performance indexes, allowing rapid comparisons of normalized data between and among differing entities.

Creating a performance measurement system

Step 1. Define needed types of performance-related information that can help achieve desired performance levels.
Step 2. Develop a relevant and usable family of measures.
Step 3. Develop specific performance measurement hierarchies.

5

Units of Measurement

Always compare apples to apples.

Two individuals go on decidedly different diets. One individual loses 18 pounds and the other loses 12 pounds. Which diet is more effective? With just this limited information, your best guess is probably the diet that resulted in a loss of 18 pounds. But what happens if you learn that the individual who lost 18 pounds was on a diet for 6 months, while the person who lost 12 pounds was on a diet for only 3 months?

Given this new information and the associated differences in the length of the diets, you would most likely need to calculate weight loss on a per-month basis to ascertain which diet is more effective. Accordingly, the person who lost 12 pounds actually lost 4 pounds per month (12/3 = 4), while the individual who lost 18 pounds only lost 3 pounds on a per-month basis (18/6 = 3). Re-examining the data this way, we might change our minds and say that the diet resulting in a 12-pound loss is apparently more effective, as measured by *pounds lost on a per-month* basis, than the diet resulting in an 18-pound loss.

Just as we might want to compare the effectiveness of two different diets, organizations often wish to compare the performance of two similar but separate entities, phenomena, etc. To do so, they must identify some common *unit of measure*. A unit of measurement is defined as a specified quantity with which any other quantity of the same kind is measured, estimated, or compared.

A common unit of measure can help an organization compare the performance of two similar entities, phenomena, etc.

For example, an oil company might want to compare exploration and production costs for different regions of the world. In this instance, it would need a common unit of measure that allows it to directly compare, for example, Canada to Africa or the United States to the Middle East. One such comparative measure on the exploration side is *finding costs*, or how much it costs to actually "find" or discover a barrel of oil (as measured by *dollars per barrel*). On the production side, a common per unit measure is *lifting costs*, or how much it costs to bring a barrel of oil to the surface (also measured on a *dollars-per-barrel* basis). Using unit measures allows direct comparisons to be made, regardless of where exploration and production activities may take place. For example, such an analysis would show that finding and lifting costs are significantly higher in Canada than they are in the Middle East. Yet an oil company might decide that these higher finding and lifting costs are offset by the much greater political stability offered in Canada as compared with that of the Middle East.

A mining company can do the same thing. To compare the richness of different gold mines regardless of geographical location, a standard unit of measurement is *ounces (of gold) per ton*. For example, a mine producing 1.2 ounces of gold per ton is decidedly richer than one producing 0.4 ounces per ton. Productivity costs, or how much it costs to mine a ton of gold ore, can also be normalized using the unit *dollars-per-ton* measure.

If we know that it costs a mining company $500 to produce 1 ton of ore, but the ore value of that same ton is only worth $450, then the mine is operating at a deficit and must either lower production costs or find a higher grade of ore. On the basis of such units of measurement information, one can directly compare two or more mines regardless of location. For example, although mine A has a higher grade (as measured by ounces per ton) than mine B, mine A's production costs (as measured by dollars per ton) are considerably higher. In this case, a lower grade of ore may be positively offset by significantly lower associated production costs.

Accordingly, per-unit measures can help us directly compare the performance of two similar but different things. They can also help an organization make better fact-based decisions—the real end goal of any performance measurement system.

> Per-unit measures can help any organization make better fact-based decisions and associated comparisons.

For example, how would you compare the performance of two different basketball scores involving four different teams? In this example, team A beat team B by a score of 108 to 103. Likewise, team C beat team D by a score of 101 to 97. Which team(s) performed better?

If we think about it for a moment, the goal of basketball is to score as many points *per possession* as possible while limiting the opposing team to as few points per possession as possible. Possessions thus represent the basic playing unit or "currency" of basketball. What happens on a *per-possession basis* ultimately determines a game's final outcome. Additionally, the number of possessions in a given game more or less equals out; that is, both teams have essentially the same number of possessions *within* a single game. However, the number of possessions *between* games can vary widely depending on the pace of the game. Some teams just run and move the ball at a faster pace than do other teams.

Accordingly, one basketball team may rank quite high in points scored on a per-possession basis, but actually lower in points scored on a per-game basis. Yet, as noted, the unit of measure of greatest importance and value is not what happens on a per-game basis, but rather what happens on a per-possession basis. As such, selecting the right unit of measure for any performance metric is of critical importance.

Selecting an appropriate unit of measure can also help us better diagnose a performance-related problem. The total time it takes to run the 100-meter dash is a good example of an outcome measure. But why does one runner beat another runner? It is primarily because one runner takes more steps per second than another runner, and/or the length of each step is longer than the other runner. Knowing both individual *steps per second* and *stride length per step* can help us better assess and perhaps improve sprinting performance.

> Selecting the right unit of measurement for any performance metric is of critical importance.

The same goes for my rowing machine. When I row a 2,000-meter piece, I get continuous information on how far I have rowed and how long it is taking me. But I also get some *per-unit* information as well, including my time (as measured in minutes and seconds) on a per-500-meter basis and my stroke count, as measured on a per-minute basis. For example, I might find that my 500-meter times and associated stroke counts are steady for about the first 1,000 meters, but they degrade significantly past that 1,000-meter distance mark. This finding suggests that I need to pace myself better in the first 1,000 meters and/or get in better shape!

Units of measure, generally expressed as "something per something else," can help us make direct performance comparisons between two different but related entities. In this regard, using a unit of measure allows any organization to make direct "apple-to-apple" comparisons. Additionally, such measures also help organizations better diagnose performance-related problems.

DEVELOPING A UNIT OF MEASURE

As noted, a unit of measure is commonly expressed as "something per something else." Examples include points scored per possession, dollars per ton, dollars per barrel, footage drilled per day, ounces per ton, calls answered per day, work orders completed per day, preventive maintenance tasks completed per week, total tonnage hauled per road mile, accidents per hundred thousand hours, and costs per student training day. Note the use of the "per" word in each case.

In developing unit measures, the first step is to identify a *meaningful measurement* unit for a particular activity or phenomena. Just as a possession is the basic playing unit or currency in basketball, an organization must determine the basic "currency" of its own operations. In some instances, such as in basketball, only a single basic unit or currency is important: a possession; however, in most other settings a number of per-unit measures may be relevant.

For example, a military airlift logistics command may want to calculate *logistics productivity*, as measured by tons of material (cargo and people) transported per day, for a particular airlift operation. To do so, the command also needs to know:

- Available aircraft: Measured by the total number of aircraft available to fly on a per day basis
- Aircraft mission load: Measured by the number of tons that an aircraft can transport per sortie

- Sorties per day: Measured by the number of sorties that an aircraft can fly per day

The actual logistics productivity formula in this instance is: *tons per day* = (number of mission aircraft available per day) × (mission tons per sortie) × (mission sorties per aircraft per day). Note that "mission tons per sortie" and "sorties per day," along with the "number of available aircraft per day" determine logistics productivity. In this example, logistics productivity is based on a number of "per-unit" measures.

Selecting the right level of a unit of measure is also important. For example, a call center might initially be interested in the number of calls processed per day. Yet a more important figure might be the number of calls processed per shift, the number of calls processed per hour, or even the number of calls processed per individual per hour. Once again, depending on the need and ultimate use of the information, selecting the right level of information is just as important as selecting the right unit of information.

Referring back to our performance measurement hierarchy as discussed in Chapter 4, lower-level measures often represent "unit measures" that aggregate upward into larger units of measure until a "whole" measure is reached at the top. Picking the right unit of measure at a lower level is critical in successfully aggregating upward until this whole is reached. In this regard, just as a performance measurement hierarchy "decomposes" as it goes down subsequent levels, it also "aggregates" as it goes up each level. Accordingly and as noted, smaller units become bigger units at higher levels until a whole is finally reached at the highest level.

SUMMARY

Organizations often wish to compare the performance of two similar but separate entities, phenomena, etc. To do so, they must identify a common unit of measure that permits them to make a direct comparison between one thing and another thing. A unit of measure is commonly expressed as "something per something else." Almost any operation or activity can be decomposed into a set of basic units that allows "something to be measured per something else." In turn, smaller units can be aggregated into larger units until a whole is reached. Unit measures can also provide considerable diagnostic value.

Creating a performance measurement system

Step 1. Define needed types of performance-related information that can help achieve desired performance levels.

Step 2. Develop a relevant and usable family of measures.

Step 3. Develop specific performance measurement hierarchies.

Step 4. Develop specific units of measure as needed.

6

Collection and Distribution

Accessibility and timeliness determine performance measure value.

Designing a performance measurement system involves answering four basic questions:

1. What?
2. Who?
3. When?
4. How?

"What" questions refer to identifying specific types of performance measures to collect. Developing a family of measures that includes critical performance factors and an associated performance measurement hierarchy, as described in Chapters 3 and 4, respectively, helps identify what specific measures to gather. Additionally, and if applicable, you should determine units of measure needed to make direct, apple-to-apple comparisons.

"Who" questions refer to identifying individuals and groups that will actually use the collected performance information. Remember, performance measures must be relevant to a particular individual or group of individuals to have real value. All too often, performance measures are collected and never used. It is imperative that actual names, titles, or functions of relevant users of the information be specifically identified and associated with each and every performance measure.

Also be sure to differentiate between an actual user and simply a "collector" of performance-related information. In many instances, such information is sent to someone who is merely charged with collecting or assembling the information. The person in turn may send it on to someone else and so forth. Such collectors and "human repositories" do not constitute relevant users. Unless a relevant user can be specifically identified by name, title, or function, collecting a proposed performance measure should be seriously questioned. When developing a performance measurement system, it is often helpful to create a matrix similar to that shown in Table 6.1. The matrix pairs at least one user name with each and every proposed performance measure.

> Always associate a specific user name (or at least function) with each and every collected performance measure.

"When" questions refer to frequency of collection and timing of distribution. Performance measures can be collected either continuously or on some predetermined intermittent sampling schedule. Continuous collection means that every event is measured. For example, cycle time and number of defects are measured on every manufactured product. Another example of continuous measurement is measuring the timeliness of every filled order.

Collecting performance information on a predetermined intermittent schedule means that only certain events are sampled. These events become

TABLE 6.1

Performance measure matrix identifying specific relevant users

Performance Measure	Specific User
BX line, activity A, cycle time	Bill (front-line supervisor)
BX line, activity A, average defects per unit	Bill (front-line supervisor)
BX line, activity B, cycle time	Sue (front-line supervisor)
BX line, activity B, average defects per unit	Sue (front-line supervisor)
BX line, activity C, cycle time	Ted (front-line supervisor)
BX line, activity C, average defects per unit	Ted (front-line supervisor)
BX line, total cycle time	Mary (line manager)
BX line, average defects per unit	Mary (line manager)

representative samples of the whole. For example, cycle time and quality-related information are collected only on every fourth product. Or in filling orders, timeliness is measured only on every tenth order. In determining sampling frequency, it is always important to let the needs of the relevant user help dictate required collection schedules.

In determining timing of distribution, it is important to know the value time frame for each performance measure and associated user. Performance-related information normally only has value for a specific time. That is why we often hear someone say, "I could have used that information 2 weeks ago. Now it is worthless." As a general rule, the closer someone is to the action (often meaning day-to-day work), the more immediate performance-related information is required.

> Normally the more someone is directly involved in a process or activity, the more immediate performance-related information is needed.

In Chapter 2, an example was cited from a service company in which front-line supervisors are able to continuously access a computer-based system to view how customer requests are queuing up. The developed system allows supervisors to instantly determine the amount of elapsed time on any given request. If an unacceptable backlog begins to accumulate, a supervisor can immediately shift work requests to other workers.

How much value would such information be to front-line supervisors if it was delivered a week later? A day later? Or even an hour later? In this instance, front-line supervisors, who are immediately controlling the action, require performance-related information in basically real time; however, their managers probably do not require such immediacy. As such, in determining timeliness of distribution, it is always important to identify who needs what when. In some instances, such as for the service company supervisors, information may be needed in near real time. Remember, performance-related information is of little value if it cannot be immediately accessed when needed.

> Performance-related information is of little value if delivered too late to the intended user.

As a general rule, when viewing a performance measurement hierarchy, collected measures normally need to be distributed much faster at the base of the hierarchy than at the top of the hierarchy. It is often beneficial to add columns for frequency of collection and timing of distribution to the matrix depicted in Table 6.1. This is illustrated in Table 6.2.

"How" questions refer to:

- How a particular performance measure is collected
- How that information is distributed to a specific person
- How the collected information is displayed (this is discussed in Chapter 7)

Answering these "how" questions before developing a matrix similar to that illustrated in Table 6.2 is extremely difficult, if not impossible. Therefore, let the developed matrix answering the what, who, and when questions also guide your collection and distribution design. For example, it is difficult to answer the question, "How do I collect cycle time?" It is much easier to answer the question, "How do I collect work order cycle time for activity B in process X and distribute that information to Mike and Jane on a weekly basis?"

TABLE 6.2

Performance measure matrix including collection frequency and distribution timing

Performance Measure	Specific User	Collection Frequency	Distribution Timing
BX line, activity A, cycle time	Bill (front-line supervisor)	Continuous (per unit)	Hourly
BX line, activity A, average defects per unit	Bill (front-line supervisor)	Continuous (per unit)	Hourly
BX line, activity B, cycle time	Sue (front-line supervisor)	Continuous (per unit)	Hourly
BX line, activity B, average defects per unit	Sue (front-line supervisor)	Continuous (per unit)	Hourly
BX line, activity C, cycle time	Ted (front-line supervisor)	Continuous (per unit)	Hourly
BX line, activity C, average defects per unit	Ted (front-line supervisor)	Continuous (per unit)	Hourly
BX line, total cycle time	Mary (line manager)	Continuous (per unit)	Daily
BX line, average defects per unit	Mary (line manager)	Continuous (per unit)	Daily

In developing the means for collecting performance measures, always attempt to "piggyback" on an existing system. For example, there may already be a work order log-in system in place for activity B of process X. The existing log-in system already identifies entry and exit times for each work order. The difference (exit time − entry time) represents work order cycle time for activity B. Instead of creating a new cycle time collection system, one simply has to collect the existing work order log-in forms and do some basic subtraction. The good news is that the work order log-in system is probably on a computer system, so a bit of simple programming can result in the needed cycle time data being collected automatically. The next task is to devise the means such that Mike and Jane can receive the information on the needed weekly basis.

> When developing a performance measurement collection process, always try to "piggyback" on an existing system as much as possible.

Also when developing a collection method, focus on collecting bottom-level performance hierarchy measures first. Frequently, measures higher in a performance hierarchy can simply be aggregated from lower measures. However, remember the cautions associated with such summing, as described in Chapter 4.

When collecting performance metrics, a little extra effort can sometimes result in the collection of a disproportionate amount of additional information. Returning to Figure 2.4, for example, one could simply click a stopwatch at the beginning and end of an obstacle course run to derive total time. This would result in an overall obstacle course outcome measure. But think how easy it is to further divide the obstacle course into various stages and interstages and collect this more detailed time-based information at the same time that you are collecting start/stop times. The same concept can be applied in any performance measurement system. Always ask yourself, "Since I am collecting this information, with a little bit of extra effort, how much more information can I collect?" Such additional information normally represents good in-process information that is particularly valuable for diagnostic purposes.

Some companies use a "hub and spoke" system for collecting and distributing performance measures. As illustrated in Figure 6.1, all collected performance measures are routed to a single individual, department, or even software program for additional processing and analysis before subsequent distribution on some predetermined schedule.

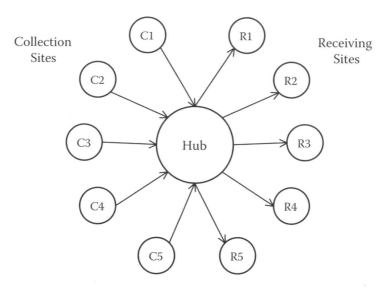

FIGURE 6.1

A typical "hub and spoke" performance measurement collection and distribution system diagram.

COLLECTION AND DISTRIBUTION SYSTEM

With advances in computer-based technologies, many companies are using networked, computer-based performance measurement collection and distribution systems. Computer-based systems in some instances can collect performance-related information in near real time and distribute this information to almost everyone simultaneously. Such systems provide process monitoring and enhanced situational awareness capabilities that simply cannot be duplicated or matched with hand-collected or paper-based distribution systems. Yet in some instances, simpler is better. Accordingly, the question should not be what high- or low-tech method will be used to collect, process, and distribute performance-related information, but rather what "right-tech" solution best meets the needs of the system and end users.

Two final columns may now be added to the matrix started in Table 6.1 and expanded upon in Table 6.2. The columns include collection and distribution methods as illustrated in Table 6.3. In most instances, the creation of a performance measurement matrix is an interactive process; that is, several changes and fine-tunings are normal. Additionally in such iterative situations, one may find that the ability to actually measure a desired

TABLE 6.3

Performance measure matrix including collection and distribution methods

Performance Measure	Specific User	Collection Frequency	Distribution Timing	Collection Method	Distribution Method
BX line, activity A, cycle time	Bill (front-line supervisor)	Continuous (per unit)	Hourly	Runtime sensors	Machine displays
BX line, activity A, average defects per unit	Bill (front-line supervisor)	Continuous (per unit)	Hourly	QA inspect	QA reports
BX line, activity B, cycle time	Sue (front-line supervisor)	Continuous (per unit)	Hourly	Runtime sensors	Machine displays
BX line, activity B, average defects per unit	Sue (front-line supervisor)	Continuous (per unit)	Hourly	QA inspect	QA reports
BX line, activity C, cycle time	Ted (front-line supervisor)	Continuous (per unit)	Hourly	Runtime sensors	Machine displays
BX line, activity C, average defects per unit	Ted (front-line supervisor)	Continuous (per unit)	Hourly	QA inspect	QA reports
BX line, total cycle time	Mary (line mgr)	Continuous (per unit)	Daily	A + B + C total time	Printout analysis
BX line, average defects per unit	Mary (line mgr)	Continuous (per unit)	Daily	A + B + C average	QA reports analysis

performance factor may prove to be impractical or simply too costly or too time consuming.

Creating such a matrix also forces designers to consider all aspects of a performance measurement system. In the end, the developed performance measurement system should be SMART (i.e., specific, measurable, actionable, relevant, and timely). In creating a collection and distribution method, timeliness should always be a key consideration. Remember, performance-related information is of little value if it cannot be immediately accessed when and where it is needed.

> Timeliness of delivery and accessibility frequently determine performance measure value and ultimate usability.

SUMMARY

The design and development of any performance measurement collection and distribution system should be guided by first identifying:

- Specific measures to be collected
- Relevant users
- Required collection frequencies and timeliness of distribution

Whenever possible, piggyback on existing information collection and distribution systems to obtain performance-related information. Also, always determine how a bit of extra collection effort may result in much greater performance-based understanding and use. Furthermore, when developing a collection and distribution system, always make sure that specific performance-related information is provided to a relevant and real user in a timely fashion such that the information actually adds value to some organization entity, be it an operation, process, activity, etc.

Creating a performance measurement system

Step 1. Define needed types of performance-related information that can help achieve desired performance levels.
Step 2. Develop a relevant and usable family of measures.
Step 3. Develop specific performance measurement hierarchies.
Step 4. Develop specific units of measure as needed.
Step 5. Develop performance measurement collection and distribution methods that ensure timeliness and usability.

7

Performance Measure Displays

A graph is worth a thousand words.

The final step in creating a performance measurement system is the actual design and development of the performance-related information displays themselves. This is basically the "how should it look" part of the performance measurement development process. The goal of any performance measure display is to provide intended users with relevant and meaningful information that can be easily and quickly assimilated and understood. Another goal is to transform the presented information into actionable knowledge on the basis of what "is" being displayed. Many companies, in an attempt to better distribute performance-related information to their employees, have adopted the concept of a visual office or factory by posting performance measure displays throughout their respective facilities.

Performance measure displays should provide relevant and meaningful information that can be quickly and easily assimilated and understood by the intended user.

For example, how would you display the status of a baseball game in real time? Figure 7.1 does just that. Note in this example, five individual display "windows" are used to capture all pertinent baseball performance-related information. The windows include (from left to right):

FIGURE 7.1
A real-time baseball performance information display.

- Team scores: In this case, team A leads team B by a score of 3 to 2.
- Inning: Represented here by the top of the third inning. The "arrow" points upward to indicate the top of the inning and downward to indicate the bottom of the inning.
- Outs: Indicated here by one out.
- Runners on base: The three diamonds signify first, second, and third base going from right to left. Note that in this example, second and third base are black, indicating that runners are currently on these two bases.
- Pitching count: Represented here by a full count of three balls (the first number) and two strikes (the second number).

By examining Figure 7.1, one can instantly get a snapshot of "what is happening" and to a certain extent "what has happened." Although the display does not provide much "why" information (who hit what when and how far), additional levels of information could be added in some embedded manner.

As illustrated in Figure 7.1, a performance-related information display should always provide relevant and meaningful information that can be quickly and easily assimilated and understood by the intended user without a great deal of study. If someone has to spend considerable time studying your performance measure display to even begin to comprehend it, then the display is probably too complex and needs to be simplified. As noted, the goal in the development of any performance-related information display is to provide relevant and meaningful information that can be quickly and easily assimilated and understood.

A dashboard-type performance measure display (illustrated in Figure 7.2) is often the easiest to comprehend and something that most of us are already used to seeing and understanding. In fact, the cluster of displays on your car's dashboard provides some interesting insights and general guidelines for creating performance measure displays. These insights and general guidelines are discussed in the following subsections.

A QUICK SCAN TELLS ALL

The displays on your car's dashboard normally do not require lengthy study to gain needed information (this would be a real safety hazard if

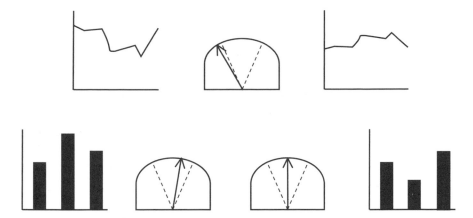

FIGURE 7.2
A conceptual performance measure display.

they did). Instead, they are designed in such a way that a quick glance provides most, if not all, of the needed information. In creating performance measure displays, this same principle should be followed. A good display arrangement should quickly provide all critically needed performance-related information to even the most casual observer. Only if problems are noted or if someone desires more "why" information should greater in-depth study be required.

Information Does Not Have to Be Further Converted or Translated

Think how disconcerting it would be if your speedometer displayed that you were traveling at 17 × 3.53 mph. You would then have to mentally make one more conversion to learn that you were actually driving about 60 mph. When creating performance measure displays, make sure that viewers will be able to quickly understand the presented information without having to first convert the data into more meaningful and relevant numbers.

Measurements Have Associated Meanings

Think for a moment about a temperature gauge on a piece of machinery in a manufacturing factory. You may not know the exact significance of a specific reading in terms of degrees Fahrenheit or Centigrade. However, such numbers are often associated with something that does have meaning, usually a color-coded system of green (normal), yellow (caution), and red (overheating or danger). As long as the numbers are in the green, you know that everything is fine or at least "normal."

The same principle applies to performance measure displays. Always attempt to provide specific meaning to individual measures by associating them with a desired performance goal (perhaps a simple dashed line) or a color-coded performance range (green for normal, yellow for caution, and red for a problem or out-of-bounds condition). The more meaning that can be provided to any performance measure display, the more beneficial it is for the intended user and the less amount of "interpretation" that is required. As such, always attempt to assist the viewer in every manner possible.

Additionally, when using color-coded schemes, always attempt to use conventional associations. For example, a green-yellow-red combination has meaning to most people; a blue-violet-pink combination does not. Although creativity and artistic license are encouraged, excesses of creativity may actually detract from the intended message. Remember, the goal of any performance measure display is to provide usable information and nothing should distract from that primary focus.

A Standardized Layout Is Developed and Maintained

What would happen, for example, if every time you glanced at your car's dashboard, the position of a specific display, like your speedometer, changed? Most of us would agree that such continued repositioning would be quite bothersome. The same concept applies to performance measure displays. As much as possible, provide consistency of place for individual display positions. This allows users to immediately direct their attention to specific information and not waste time searching from chart to chart. If a hierarchy-type display is being used, then you should naturally flow information from higher (top) to lower (bottom), more detailed levels of information.

Following the simple principles outlined above will add a great deal of value to any performance measure display. An overriding design principle in the creation of performance measure displays is that they are simple, yet intuitively informative, requiring little extra study.

> Performance measure displays should be simple, yet highly informative for the intended user.

GRAPHICAL DISPLAYS

In most instances, a graphical interface composed of various charts and graphs is used in the display of performance measures. Remember, just like a picture, a well-designed chart or graph is worth a thousand words. Although specific designs may vary, the following guiding principles should be adhered to:

- Do not make individual charts and graphs too busy. Keep them as simple as possible such that they have immediate meaning to the intended user. Although many software graphics packages provide an incredible array of features, simple and less are always better.
- Use standard types of graphs (e.g., bar charts, pie charts, line charts, etc.) that everyone is familiar with. In creating various graphs, try to maintain some sort of format consistency; that is, each graph should not be a unique design in and of itself. For example, all bar graphs should essentially look the same. Once again, do not make the intended viewer have to "translate" one graph form to another. If good is an upward trend, then as much as possible, keep good as "up."
- Use large enough font and drawing sizes such that charts and graphs can be easily read. Also make sure that you do not mistakenly fool users by adopting various scales of essentially the same phenomena. By doing so, a casual glance may indicate that one performance measure or department is doing much better or worse than another, when in fact the perceived difference is really due to using different scales. Just as there are "lies, damn lies, and statistics," there are also sometimes "creatively" crafted graphs and charts.
- As noted earlier, place meaning into graphs and charts by using commonly associated colors or desired performance goals indicated by a dashed line. When using different colors, make sure that usage is consistent and each color has a specific meaning. For example, do not use red on one graph to indicate a problem and then use it on the next graph to indicate superior performance. Also, always use the same color to represent a department or function. If the accounting department is represented by dark gray on one line graph, then it should be dark gray on other graphs and charts as well. Once again, always strive for consistency.

- Check with intended users. Get their feedback and implement their suggestions as much as possible. Remember, the intended user is the consumer of any performance measurement system and associated display. If it does not work for them, then it does not work.
- When posting performance information displays on walls and other easily observable areas, make sure that inquisitive eyes, especially those of visitors, cannot gather sensitive information about an organization. Although it is important to display collected performance measures, it is also important to ensure that the wrong people do not see company-sensitive information.

Consistency, simplicity, understandability, readability, and adequate protection should always guide the creation of any performance measure display. In many instances, excessive artistic creativity may actually distract from the intended use and understanding of a performance measure display.

For example, one company had a very creative person assigned to developing its performance measurement dashboards. The individual viewed the assignment as an opportunity for artistic expression. Each performance measure display became an individual piece of art. No two displays ever looked exactly alike. There was no standardization of color, scale, or format. Although the end product of such efforts may have been artistically interesting and aesthetically pleasing, the displays had little practical value for harried managers trying to quickly detect any change in performance or identify the root causes of a developing performance-related issue. Unfortunately, rather than change and standardize the display design process, thereby curbing such artistic license, the company did nothing. As a result, potential users simply ignored abstract displays, completely bypassing what could have potentially been a very valuable source of performance-related information.

DISPLAY ORGANIZATION

In developing performance measure displays, always think of who needs what performance-related information when and in what format. This concept applies whether the information is presented in real time via a computer-based system, a daily paper-based system, or a monthly wall-type display. One approach is to provide the most critical and/or most frequently used information in the most dominant or proximal position possible (think of how your speedometer dominates your car's dashboard). Accordingly, any graphical display—be it a computer display or a paper display in a three-ring binder—should always include the most critical information at the very beginning. Conversely, if a wall-mounted panel-type display is used, then this critical information should appear in the center of the display and be appropriately highlighted.

Additional supporting performance-related information would then be linked or embedded in this core information. Usually for panel-type displays, the supporting information is placed around the core information, as shown in Figure 7.3. In this example, core or critical measures are displayed in the center and encircled by a dashed line. Other measures of less immediate importance are outside of the dashed circle. A quick glance at the core measures should give a good overall perspective. If problems are indicated or a deeper understanding is desired, then the peripherally displayed performance measures should provide the needed information.

If supporting performance-related information is used, always attempt to graphically link it to core information whenever possible. For example,

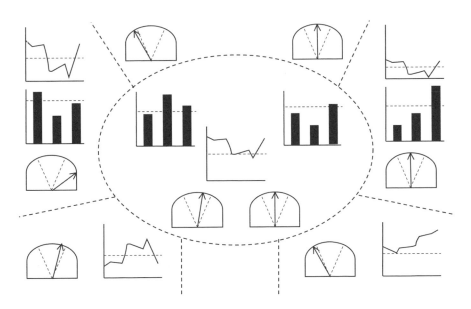

FIGURE 7.3
Core measures in a conceptual performance measure display.

if a critical process cycle time measure is based on the combined cycle time measurements of three embedded activities, then link this activity-specific information in such a way that the intended user can quickly access it (Figure 7.4). Figure 7.4 illustrates how a process-level performance measure (process X) is decomposed into three activity-level measures (A, B, and C), indicating that process X is comprised of the sum of measures from activities A, B, and C.

As noted, computer-based systems are increasingly being used to capture and display performance-related information, especially real-time information. It is important that designers of such systems avail themselves of proven techniques specifically related to good graphical user interface design. A challenge in the design of any computer-based system is the organization and "layering" of the information itself. Ideally, such performance-related information can be quickly accessed and linked to other required information. Unfortunately, becoming lost within a computer-based system while attempting to "drill-down" to lower levels of information is a continuing problem that, to date, is not completely resolved. In some ways, the design and development of static and paper-based performance measure displays is actually easier when compared to equivalent computer-based systems.

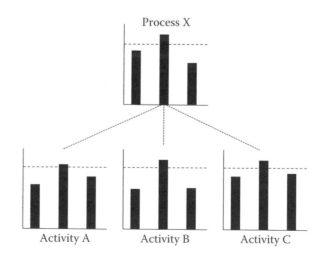

FIGURE 7.4
Linking core and supporting performance-related information.

SUMMARY

The final step in the development of a performance measurement system is the actual design of the performance-related information displays. The goal in the development of such displays is to provide specific, relevant, and usable information to the intended user. In addition, this information should be in a format that is easily and rapidly assimilated and understood. Normally graphs and charts are used in displaying performance-related information. In creating such graphics, the challenge is to provide as much meaning as possible while keeping each individual display as simple as possible. In organizing and displaying performance measures, a dashboard-type concept often proves most useful for an intended viewing audience.

Creating a performance measurement system

Step 1. Define needed types of performance-related information that can help achieve desired performance levels.
Step 2. Develop a relevant and usable family of measures.
Step 3. Develop specific performance measurement hierarchies.
Step 4. Develop specific units of measure as needed.
Step 5. Develop a performance measurement collection and distribution methods that ensure timeliness and usability.
Step 6. Develop all performance-related information displays.

8

Interpretation and Action

| From performance data to performance meaning. |

In a graphical sense, a discrete performance measure is basically represented by a "mark" on a line, bar, column, scatter plot, or similar chart. The mark in turn represents the intersection of some y and x value. Although such marks have significance in and of themselves, it is the interpretation of the mark and what is (or is not) done with that interpretation that truly adds value to any performance measurement system. Remember, the ultimate goal in measuring performance is to translate performance data into performance knowledge and associated meaning that in turn is effectively and successfully acted upon. In short, performance measurement systems should drive fact-based decision-making. As such, performance-based facts should drive performance-based actions.

| Performance-based facts should drive performance-based actions. |

A long time ago, automobile manufacturers decided that gas is a critical performance "oomph" factor for the continued operation of a car. Accordingly they developed a gas-related performance measure display, called it a gas gauge, and stuck it in a prominent position on the dashboard of every car coming out of the factory. You and I as car drivers routinely monitor that gas performance display. When the needle approaches the "E," or empty mark, we know that it is time to improve the condition of our gas tank by filling it back up. Although in such instances we may not know the exact quantity of gas remaining in our gas tank (or even how much our gas tank holds in total), we do know that whatever it is, it is insufficient if we wish to drive further.

In this example, automobile manufacturers identified a critical performance factor and then created an associated performance measure that we as drivers easily understand. That understanding allows us to take the appropriate action (fill gas tank) at the appropriate time. Any performance measurement system should do essentially the same thing. It should allow us to act at the appropriate time by capturing and measuring critical performance factors. However, executing such actions is predicated on our ability to successfully interpret and understand displayed performance data—to translate those data into some type of a performance-specific meaning. In the following sections, a few general guiding principles for interpreting performance-related data are offered.

FOCUS ON WHAT IS TRULY IMPORTANT

A large commercial training company hands out evaluation forms at the end of each of its training sessions. The company uses a five-point Liekert scale with 5 being "excellent" and 1 being "poor." Interested primarily in the perceived quality of its offered training courses, the company asks attendees to rate each course along five quality-related dimensions:

1. The overall quality of the training course (an overall, summative-type rating)
2. The quality of the instruction
3. The quality of the training materials
4. The quality of the training exercises
5. The quality of the training facilities, equipment, etc.

Such evaluations represent affective judgments, or "what did I think" evaluations by attending students.

The company is further divided into separate business units. Each business unit conducts training for a very unique client set. Each business unit also closely monitors end-of-course ratings, translating individual course averages into cumulative averages of all delivered courses.

Running cumulative averages across multiple courses within two different business units are illustrated in Figure 8.1. In examining Figure 8.1, one may instantly note that business unit B seems to be doing a better job

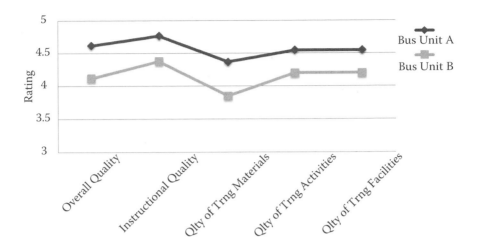

FIGURE 8.1
Cumulative average ratings of delivered training courses by business unit.

of training its respective clientele than is business unit A. But is this really true?

The measurement of human perception as opposed to actual quantity-related measures can sometimes be a bit fickle. One group may naturally rate the exact same thing higher or lower than another group. For example, within-company surveys often depict higher ratings by managers, mid-level ratings by professional white-collar workers, and lower ratings by blue-collar labor workers. In such "differential" instances, what is often more important is not the "between" ratings but the "within" ratings, that is, how one group compares different "within" dimensions when compared to another group. Using this "within" perspective, we often find manager-, white-collar, and blue-collar ratings surprisingly similar.

Examining Figure 8.1 a bit closer, one sees that the within ratings of the two graph forms are almost identical. Note that the highest marks within each business unit are given for "instructional quality." Note also the relatively sharp decrease in the quality of "training materials" for both business units. In turn, the quality of "training activities" and "training facilities" once again increases for both groups when compared with the quality of "training materials."

Examining Figure 8.1 in this light, where should you direct any performance improvement effort? The answer is fairly obvious, is it not? Although the between graph forms illustrated in Figure 8.1 are somewhat different, the within ratings tell the exact same story—the quality of training materials needs to be improved. Accordingly, the company should direct any improvement effort toward improving the quality of its training materials.

When attempting to interpret a graph, chart, or other type of performance measure display, always ask yourself what is of critical importance. By better understanding what is normal (different groups can perceive things differently) and what is not normal (the perceived quality of training materials should not be significantly different than the perceived quality of any other performance dimension), you can better interpret a performance-related graph form.

KNOW WHEN TO HOLD

Performance often improves in a very predictable manner. Slow growth or improvement gives way to rapid growth, followed once again by slowed growth, which eventually transforms into no growth. This slow growth, fast growth, slowed growth, no growth performance improvement life cycle results in a very characteristic S-shaped looking performance curve, as illustrated in Figure 8.2. Although in the real world such curves are rarely perfectly S-shaped, they nevertheless routinely have an S-shaped look to them.

When an organization launches a performance improvement effort, they often expect immediate, rapid, and dramatic gains in performance from the outset. Yet the introduction of a new performance improvement "innovation"—be it a new technology, process, procedure, etc.—often immediately results in no gain or only a small, incremental gain at best. In fact, sometimes a slight loss in performance is observed. Disappointed with such initial results or the lack thereof, organizations often prematurely abandon their new improvement effort. In turn, anti-improvement naysayers within the organization issue "I told you so" statements that often negate any future performance improvement efforts as well.

As illustrated in Figure 8.2, the bottom of any S-shaped performance curve is fairly flat and unimpressive. Yet it often portends the start of

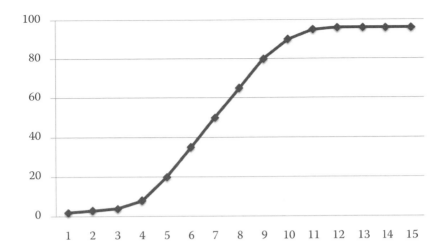

FIGURE 8.2
A characteristic S-shaped performance curve.

something much more exciting; accordingly, be patient. Although initial associated performance improvement measures may not be as spectacular as you envisioned, given enough time, slow growth often (but certainly not always) transforms into rapid growth. Accordingly, always know when to hold!

RESPECT THE TURTLE

Performance often improves in an incremental fashion. Although dramatic gains in performance certainly do occur, they often occur much less than we might wish to think. They also occur much less than what performance consultants often promise their respective and sometimes naive and unsuspecting client sets.

Although a fairly steep rise in performance is illustrated in Figure 8.2, a closer examination reveals that the rise is composed of a series of incremental gains that cumulatively create the steep part of the curve. As depicted in Figure 8.2, a fairly dramatic performance improvement effort when examined closely is almost always comprised of a series of incremental gains that individually may not be all that impressive. Yet the summation of these individual gains over time can result in some fairly dramatic "results." Understanding this often-observed incremental growth form allows us to offer countenance and patience to impatient general managers demanding spectacular improvements in performance. Persistence, a respect for the turtle, and an understanding of S-curves are thus critical to the success of any sustained performance improvement effort.

KNOW WHEN TO FOLD

In performance S-shaped curve speak, what goes up eventually flattens out. The top, flat part of the S is called an asymptote. It often represents a performance limit or wall, signifying that the amount of performance improvement potential in a given system has essentially been depleted or tapped out. Accordingly, doing more of the same rarely results in any additional or significant result. Instead, doing more of the same needlessly consumes precious resources. Although a performance improvement method may have worked quite well in the past (during the steep rise of the S), those days are unfortunately over.

When an asymptote is reached, organizations should certainly ensure that accrued gains in performance are successfully maintained and do not degrade over time; however, they should not exert much effort or spend a great deal of money in attempting to increase performance using old and supposedly tried and proven methods. Instead, it is time to try something new. If an organization is successful in implementing something new, it will essentially begin the performance improvement process anew. With time, this success is reflected in a performance curve that resembles multiple S-shaped curves, one "stacked" on top of the other (see Figure 8.3).

In this regard, an earlier S-shaped slow growth, rapid growth, slowed growth, no growth performance improvement life cycle gives way to a later and newer improvement cycle, but one initially marked by only the next, new slow growth phase. However, hopefully with time this slow growth second cycle phase will give way to a more rapid growth phase, accruing significant gains in performance once again.

As described in previous chapters, performance measurement systems can tell us a great deal about what is happening and what has happened. They can also tell us something about what may happen. Yet all of this "telling" is based on our ability to correctly interpret such measures; that

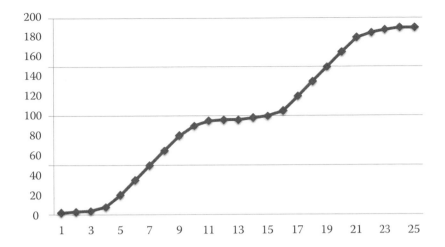

FIGURE 8.3
A series of S-shaped performance curves.

is, it is based on our ability to correctly translate performance data into performance meaning. The more we collectively know about performance and how it does and does not improve, the more our collective interpretations will have real meaning and be able to drive fact-based decisions and associated actions. Just as performance measurement systems increase our ability to manage, control, and improve something, they also increase our ability to understand something.

SUMMARY

The ultimate goal of any performance measurement system is to translate performance data into performance knowledge and meaning, which in turn are effectively and successfully acted upon. In short, performance-based facts should drive performance-based actions. However, a prerequisite condition for all of this "performance-based" stuff is correctly interpreting performance data in the first place. The more we collectively know about performance and how it does and does not improve, the more such collective interpretations will have real meaning and allow us to make better performance-based decisions.

9

Putting It All Together

> Up-front design equals downstream value and action.

A critical enabler in creating and maintaining a high-performance organization is the ability to quantitatively measure performance. Such an accrued ability allows any organization to transition from making subjective, opinion-based decisions to making objective, fact-based decisions. In essence, such organizations let derived performance-based facts drive subsequent performance-based actions.

In the previous chapters, the following general steps for creating a performance measurement system were identified and described:

1. *Define the types of performance-related information needed to achieve desired performance levels.* Such measures commonly include descriptive-, diagnostic-, and predictive-type measures. These various types of measures are not mutually exclusive, and a single measure can serve multiple roles. The goal in developing any performance measurement system is to create measures that have real value and meaning and are action-oriented.

2. *Develop a relevant and usable family of measures.* Developing a family of measures helps an organization identify those few, but oh-so-important "oomph" factors that critically drive performance, thus allowing any organization to focus on the critical few instead of the trivial many. A family of measures usually represents four to six interrelated but separate key aspects of performance. They normally involve the following types of measures: productivity, quality, timeliness, cycle time, resource utilization, cost, and safety. In

many instances, multiple measures of the same family member are collected.

3. *Develop specific performance measurement hierarchies.* A performance measurement hierarchy consists of different levels of the same performance measure (e.g., cycle time for specific activities comprising a higher-level process). The creation of a performance measurement hierarchy helps ensure that relevant and meaningful performance-related information is collected and distributed within the right levels of an organization. As noted, providing the right level of information to the right person(s) at the right time is critical for optimizing overall organizational performance. In creating a performance measurement hierarchy, specific users should always be associated with each measurement level. This practice ensures that the right person is receiving the right level of performance-related information.

4. *Develop specific units of measure as needed.* Often performance measures are used to compare and contrast two separate entities. Yet to make such comparisons, a common unit of measure is necessary. A unit of measurement is defined as a specified quantity with which any other quantity of the same kind is measured, estimated, or compared. In short, a common unit of measure allows apple-to-apple comparisons. Units of measure are commonly expressed as "something per something else."

5. *Develop collection and distribution methods that ensure timeliness and usability.* To achieve relevance and associated value, most performance-related information must have timeliness. Creating collection and distribution methods that provide relevant information to specific users within a required time frame is critical to the ultimate success of any performance measurement system. Increasingly, a usable time frame means almost near real time. Accordingly, computer-based systems have much to offer in the collection and distribution of performance-related measures. Yet in the end, "right tech" will always trump "high tech." Additionally, when initially developing performance measure collection and distribution strategies, piggyback on existing systems whenever possible.

6. *Develop useful performance-related information displays.* The actual output of any performance measurement system is often a graphical display such as a chart or graph of a set of performance measures.

A key factor in successfully developing such displays is that they are simple, comprehensible, meaningful, and above all else usable for the intended user. Better displays can be developed by always incorporating user feedback and associated needs. Finally, just as it is important to determine "what" performance measures to display, it is equally important to determine "what not" to display, especially if such information is company sensitive or of a proprietary nature.

By giving careful consideration to the initial design and development of a performance measurement system, more meaningful, usable, actionable, and true value-added performance-related information can be obtained. Always remember the SMART acronym, developing performance measures that are specific, measurable (quantitatively), actionable, relevant, and timely.

A review of the following guidelines can help in the design of any performance measurement system:

- *Measurement drives behavior.* This can be good or bad. Make sure, then, that you measure the things that will actually help achieve desired performance objectives. Developing bad measures that can be easily manipulated or that lead to unwanted performance outcomes (e.g., holding team meetings for no real purpose except that the number of team meetings held is being tracked) adds little value to any organization.

- *Measure both the "ends" of performance and the "means" for accomplishing those ends.* Remember, performance is captured by the formula $y = f(x)$, or outcome y is a function of variable set x. Accordingly, you need to measure outcomes and the means for achieving those outcomes. A family of measures should thus always include the critical x values that drive organizational performance, as well as associated outcome y measures.

- *Always measure the critical few and not the trivial many: Performance measurement systems cost money to develop and maintain, and such resources should never be wasted.* As noted, focus on capturing those critical measures that drive performance and will actually be used (by a real person).

- *To ensure usefulness and relevance, tie a specific performance measure to a specific user by name or position.* An acid test of any performance measurement system should be the ability to identify by name who uses what information and how it is being used to achieve what supporting goal.

- *Develop measures and associated capture/delivery systems that provide adequate warnings of unwanted changes.* To have relevance, such information must also have timeliness; that is, it cannot be delivered or gathered after the fact. Remember, a good performance measurement system provides the right kinds of information to the right people at the right time in the right format.
- *Performance measure displays should be easily and quickly understandable.* Keep displays simple, specific, and relevant. Graphical forms are best, in that a chart is worth a thousand words.
- *Performance improvement often follows a fairly predictable, S-shaped curve life cycle: Initial slow growth gives way to rapid growth, only to be replaced by slowed growth, which eventually results in no growth.* Understanding how performance does and does not improve is critical to correctly interpreting many performance-related graphs. It is important in any performance improvement effort to know when to hold and when to fold.

SUMMARY

Companies are increasingly transitioning from management by opinion to management by hard fact and concrete evidence. They are collecting real numbers and using those numbers to set, monitor, and achieve desired performance levels. A key enabler in this transition from opinion- to fact-based management is the development of a supporting performance measurement system. A performance measurement system is normally a graphical and numerical information system (often referred to as a performance dashboard or scorecard) used to monitor, assess, diagnose, and achieve desired performance levels. A performance measurement system involves defining, developing, collecting, synthesizing, delivering, and displaying performance-related information in an intuitive and understandable fashion. Such systems should always capture both outcome- and means (or in-process)-related performance information. The ultimate goal of any performance measurement system is to translate collected and displayed performance data into performance knowledge and meaning, which in turn are effectively and successfully acted upon: that is, performance-based facts should always drive performance-based actions. Accordingly, collected performance measures should be SMART: specific, measurable, actionable, relevant, and timely.

Performance measures can be used for several different purposes and can answer varying types of performance-related questions. Regardless of the types of measures used, a good performance measurement system should always provide:

- Descriptive value: Describing what is happening and has happened.
- Diagnostic value: Assisting us in better understanding why something is happening or has happened.
- Predictive value: Helping us infer what may happen (but to date has not happened).

Descriptive, diagnostic, and predictive performance measures thus aid in better understanding, managing, and improving the performance levels of our respective organizations. In short, you really can't understand, manage, or improve what you don't (quantitatively) measure.

Further Reading

Brown, M. G. *Keeping Score: Using the Right Metrics to Drive World Class Performance*. New York: Productivity Press, 2006.

Brown, M. G. *Beyond the Balanced Scorecard: Implementing Business Intelligence with Analytics*. New York: Productivity Press, 2007.

Christopher, W., and C. Thor, eds. *Handbook for Productivity Measurement and Improvement*. New York: Productivity Press, 1993 (includes several articles by Carl Thor).

Harbour, J. L. *Basics of Performance Measurement*, 1st ed. New York: Productivity Press, 1997.

Harbour, J. L. *The Performance Paradox: Understanding the Real Drivers that Critically Affect Outcomes*. New York: Productivity Press, 2008.

Index

A

Accessibility, 55, 61
Accounting, 34–35
Action, 73–79
Analysis, 31
As-is measurements. *See* Baseline
    measurement
Asymptote, 5, 8, 78

B

Baseline measurement, 2, 6, 8, 14–15
Business process reengineering, 1

C

Charts, 2–4, 19, 21, 42, 67, 71. *See also*
    Displays
Collection, 15, 30, 42–43, 55–62
Color coding, 66, 67
Comparisons, 29–30, 55
    performance indexes, 45–46
    units of measurement, 49–54
Computers, 60, 70
Conceptual performance measure display,
    65
Consistency, 66–68
Continuous improvement, 1
Continuous measurement, 56
Control measures, 21
Core measures, 69–70
Correlated measures, 32–34
Cost measurement, 8
Costs, 5, 28, 34, 36, 50
Critical measures. *See* Family of measures
Critical performance factor, 74
Customer service, 3, 8, 35
Cycle time, 1-9, 16, 18, 19, 28, 34, 40–41,
    56

D

Data collection, 4–5, 15, 55. *See also*
    Collection
Delta, 2, 6
Descriptive measures, 8, 14–17, 21, 24, 40
Design of displays, 66–68
Diagnostic measurements, 8, 14, 17–21,
    24, 40
Displays, 30–31, 55–62, 63–74
Distribution, 7, 30–31, 55–62
Documentation, 1–3

E

Economic concerns, 5
Engineering, 35
Evaluation, 8
Extraction businesses, 35

F

Family of measures, 8, 25–38, 55
Frequency, 56–58, 61

G

Gap, 2, 6
Goals, 2, 6, 9, 13, 30, 63
Graphs, 2–4, 15, 19. *See also* Displays

H

Healthcare, 35
Hierarchy, 10, 31, 39–47, 53, 55, 57, 66
Hub and spoke, 59–60
Human Development Index (HDI), 45

I

Immaturity, 22–23

Author

Dr. Jerry Harbour combines over 30 years of domestic and international experience from such diverse fields as advanced technology development and evaluation, defense and national security, national laboratory research and development, oil exploration and production, underground mining, and training development and delivery. He is the author of *The Performance Paradox: Understanding the Real Drivers that Critically Affect Outcomes*. Jerry and his wife, along with their golden retriever, divide their time between living in New Mexico and Colorado.